MEDITATIONS ON FREEDOM
AND THE SPIRIT

Meditations on Freedom and the Spirit

KARL RAHNER

A Crossroad Book
THE SEABURY PRESS • NEW YORK

1978
The Seabury Press
815 Second Avenue
New York N.Y. 10017

Printed in the United States of America

Library of Congress Cataloging in Publication Data

Rahner, Karl, 1904-   Meditations on freedom and the spirit.
"A Crossroad book."
CONTENTS: Faith as courage. — Freedom and manipulation in
society and the church. — Toleration in the church.
1. Faith — Addresses, essays, lectures. 2. Courage — Addresses,
essays, lectures. 3. Freedom (Theology) — Addresses, essays,
lectures. 4. Liberty of speech in the church — Addresses, essays,
lectures. 5. Sociology, Christian (Catholic) — Addresses, essays,
lectures. I. Title.
BV4637.R34213   234'.2   78-50895
ISBN 0-8164-2162-5

Contents

Page

PART ONE: FAITH AS COURAGE

Foreword   7

I   Words as keys to existence   9

II   Courage in hope   12

III Radical total courage   15

IV   Courage as faith   19

V   Courage as Christian faith   24

PART TWO: FREEDOM AND
MANIPULATION IN SOCIETY AND THE
CHURCH

Foreword   33

I   The concept of freedom   36

II   Freedom and manipulation in society   48

III Freedom and manipulation in the
     Church   57

IV   Freedom and love   63

PART THREE: TOLERATION IN THE
CHURCH

Foreword   75

I   Conflicts   81

II   Doctrine and authority   97

III Practice and toleration   110

PART ONE: FAITH AS COURAGE

Foreword

The theme of this section seemed, when it was first suggested to me, an unusual and surprising subject for reflection. Yet it is one on which I am glad to have an opportunity to present my thoughts. Contrary to many current views, our Christian faith is fundamentally simple (and difficult only in its simplicity), because it is the practical expression of what we may call 'courage'. Needless to say, the word 'courage', as it is used here, must be understood in a truly radical sense and in relation to the whole of human existence.

I Words as keys to existence

I make no claim to be an expert in the field of linguistic philosophy, yet I feel that a distinction may justifiably be drawn between two groups of nouns. Words in the first group have a clearly defined sense which can be clarified and classified ever more precisely and scientifically, a sense which is clearly differentiated from that of other words. 'Hydrogen', 'cockroach', and 'house' are good examples of such words. They define and delimit a quite precise single real object in the complexity of our empirical experience of the world.

There is, however, a second, very different group of words, which are not similarly clear and precise, although they cannot therefore be denied meaning and validity. They are words which start from a definite point of human experience, but do not define or differentiate. If the radical nature of their meaning is recognized, however, they are seen to hold the key to the whole of man's existence and the reality of life. They are words which relate specifically to human life, which are concerned with man as a whole — man whose spirit and freedom are constantly stretching out beyond the trivial and limited nature of the finite reality within his empirical experience, until finally he is lost in that mysterious darkness which embraces and enfolds all human existence.

The rational positivist may say that such words are unscientific and have no place in science or sober philosophy, where poetic language is out of place; silence is the only possible response where a clear statement is impossible; clear, that is, in the sense of being unambiguously verifiable. But is it possible to be human and to live a human life, if words like freedom, love, loyalty, joy, responsibility, fear, and so on are to be avoided? Surely it is impossible. But such words are lost in the total sum of human experience, even though they start from a definite point of meaning. Their meaning cannot be established precisely like the meaning of factual aspects of reality, which have a definite place within man's life and man's world. For this whole existence of man is given into his charge, whole and entire, for always; so he cannot simply dismiss the matter out of irritation or depression as 'incomprehensible' or 'incapable of precise definition'. He is inescapably concerned with the totality of his existence at any and every point when he makes a free and responsible decision, when he asks questions knowing that he does so, and that this is a responsibility he cannot abdicate, no matter whether he is conscious of this intuitively or 'forgets' it or dismisses it, while he occupies himself with some specific subject, which is itself clear or can be explained 'scientifically'.

A man can always let himself be so busy that he is rushed through the multifarious activities of his life, through the individual experiences and individual influences connected with them. He can always forget *himself* in his concern with the thousand and one details he has to deal with and so in the field of language he can always *try* to limit himself to that first group of words, as far as he is able. But he will never really become free of himself in this way. The totality, the oneness of his existence, which he is trying to push away and forget in his daily life, will always rise from the background gloom to which it has been consigned and constantly put before him and his freedom the ultimate question of how he relates to this totality, what he intends to make of it and not just of the thousand details of his life. So in a real life of freedom and responsibility no one can live only with the words of the first group, which are those of the so-called exact sciences. If he once asks what science and truth themselves are, he falls inevitably into the sphere of this mysterious second group of words, which prove unavoidable, even if he denies them the characteristic of scientific clarity and non-ambuity.

It is among these unavoidable words, which open up the mysterious totality of human existence, that the word 'courage' belongs. My aim here is to show how courage, understood in its existential necessity and radical nature, is in fact what is called faith in Christian theology.

II Courage in hope

A few preliminary comments are perhaps needed to clarify my intentions and remove any possible misunderstandings. As has already been said, the words belonging to the second group refer to human existence in all its aspects. When we talk about freedom, we mean something different from when we talk about responsibility. Joy and fear, despair and hope see man's uniqueness from very different vantage-points, describe different aspects of it, just as man's own basic freedom is in constant contrast with the single totality of existence. But because each of these words relates to man in his uniqueness and his unfettered questioning and activity, these words always overlap, each assimilating the meaning of the other (in approbation or negation); so they are neither merely synonyms nor yet clearly demarcated one from the other. It is precisely this remarkable relationship of such words with one another, which presents the possibility of establishing 'key-concepts' in the intellectual and spiritual history of mankind. Such key-concepts are intended to provide an insight into the mysterious unity of human existence, but they do so from very different starting-points; they are different and yet merge into one another when they

are understood in a truly radical sense. Without necessarily evoking the totality of man's existence, which is
their ultimate task, they can either exist side by side or
alternate with one another.

Three of these key-concepts, at least, are very familiar
to a Christian: faith, hope and love. All three have their
source in the New Testament, but the stress is different
according to the book, so that often an understanding
of one key concept illuminates another. It is true that
Catholic theology (particularly Tridentine theology)
made as clear a distinction as possible between these
three concepts of basic human and Christian development and tried to interpret them as consecutive phases
of one fundamental progression, which came to maturity
through these phases. This is still a perfectly valid interpretation. But in the final analysis it becomes increasingly
clear that all three words encompass the complete progression of Christian existence, each in itself alone. Each
one of these three words is seen in its full radical meaning
only when it is 'subsumed' into the two other words.

In the New Testament there are, of course, other such
key concepts which also belong to the second group of
words: freedom, *logos*, light, truth, spirit, grace, reconciliation, peace, justice and so on. All these concepts are
or can be key concepts. Their fate has been a variable
one in the course of the history of Christian thought,
since they have naturally not been equally effective as a
means of revealing the totality of human existence in
every period of history with its own particular character.
Hence in the history of Christian spirituality up to the
present day there have been words which came from the
dimension of man's knowledge of himself or of his
individual salvation and performed this function of
revelation for men of an earlier time, such as *logos*,
truth, direct vision of God, love, justification.

Today, in the era of creative freedom and openness
towards the future, such words and phrases as universal

justice, emancipation, and hope can be similar key concepts of an effective kind. Such new key-concepts do not simply replace the old ones but, correctly and radically understood, themselves illuminate the earlier terms. To have a true and radical hope is to have faith and love also, because a necessary constituent of hope is an impulse towards knowledge of faith and hope itself only comes to fruition when hope is felt as part of love for our fellow human beings.

If in our day hope is the 'principle', the key concept, the preferred word among the words of the second group we spoke of initially, then the word 'courage' is one that comes close to it. For ultimately courage is hope, and hope would be nothing if it were not courageous. I reflect on the word 'courage' not in order to lend it the dignity of a time-honoured key-term in Christian life for each and every person. It is rather that the concept of *hope* can be better and more radically understood from the concept of courage. It can thus become clearer how far removed hope is from being a flight from reality, the cheap consolation or even the opium of the people that it always runs the danger of seeming. It can become clearer that hope is decision, action and risk: and these are attributes of the person of courage. Then it can and should be seen how such courageous hope, such courage in hope, when radical enough, are in fact what Christian theology terms faith, in the strict meaning of the word. There is no doubt that such faith, which is already an integral part of this courage, has to become part of actual Christian belief and be put into practice if it is to reach its own essential fulness.

III Radical total courage

Courage is hard to define. Not because we do not recognize it when we see it, but because it cannot be defined and delimited as a specific fact, in the sense that the first group of words I mentioned can: it is a way of living, which characterizes the whole man. This courage is concerned with man's whole existence, since it shares the impossibility of an adequate reflection and definition of this existence. The courage that is meant here is not courage for this or that particular act a person may do, but courage in and for oneself in the whole sphere of human life.

Perhaps only through examples can courage be described and made part of man's active consciousness. Courage is not devoid of uncertainty, of fear of failure in attaining a freely chosen and desired goal, of determination. Courage certainly can, even should, co-exist with planning, with working out the chances of success. But where courage is really required is when there is a gap for rational consideration between the calculation of the possibilities of success and the actual performance of the task, where success is not known for certain before it is actually achieved. This inevitable gulf, which exists in all cases of calculations made beforehand between the aim or purpose and the prospects for its success, is filled by what I shall call hoping courage: the courage of hope. The gulf between the action which cannot be calculated in advance and the action itself is bridged by courage.

The rational man today has certainly the right and the duty in his activities and undertakings of working out his calculations in advance as accurately and with as much certainty as possible. He has to reduce the gap as far as possible before he acts, to the point where there seems practically no need for courage for the action. A civil engineer, for example, knows with practically perfect assurance in advance of a bridge's completion that it will hold and that therefore no courage is required to proceed with the building. But in thousands of human activities the gap remains, the intended outcome cannot be calculated precisely in advance, so that it is identical with the result achieved and it is impossible to find out or know adequately all the factors involved in a situation. When action must nonetheless be taken, then courage is indispensable. This is even true in everyday life with its thousand and one activities. It is especially true in those cases where the action and the courage for the action concern the totality of a man's existence. This is the courage we have to consider.

The fact that such radical and total courage exists and inevitably must exist, naturally presupposes that in our lives as human beings we are concerned not just with this and that, with the thousand private objectives of our existence, with our partner, the dictates of our work, our holidays and our personal problems, but with ourselves as whole persons and individuals. This essential condition for the concept of courage, as it is envisaged above, cannot be justified more precisely here. We presume that man as an individual is not concerned just with a vast mass of details in his life, through which he drives himself or is driven. He has to realize himself as a whole person in and through all these individual episodes of his life, whether he knows it consciously or not. Because of his freedom man is himself, by definition, both subject and object. He has not only a great number and variety of things to do in his life, but has to be concerned about himself as an individual, a task which in theological language we call his salvation. He can obliterate or suppress this first and last task in the many many aspects of his life. He can change from the personal 'I' to the impersonal 'one'. But even when it is suppressed or forgotten, the feeling is still there, the feeling of being concerned for himself, of being condemned to freedom, of being ultimately responsible for himself. It is felt most strongly in periods of loneliness and ultimate decision, in the challenge to accept a final responsibility which no one will applaud.

In developing this line of thought I hope to show more clearly still what is meant by total radical courage. Man is wholly and completely himself in his freedom, even for his first and last task. Yet he knows at the same time that the fulfilment of this one task depends upon a thousand other conditions and causes, which he cannot foresee and which are not under his control. Moreover he experiences his own freedom as limited and threatened; he feels that the most personal aspects of his individuality are mysteriously alien to him.

For both these reasons we see here in the most radical and irreversible form that gulf between the active individual with his ability, his power, his means of calculating in advance on the one hand and on the other hand what has to be done in a specific real-life situation: the ultimate, final, personal decision as a completion of the unlimited possibilities which are given as spirit and freedom to man; the final self-realization that a man does not merely accept passively but gives himself actively and creatively. He experiences this gulf precisely because he is at one and the same time a creature of unlimited ambitions, a man who can never remain satisfied by a limited goal; and yet he also feels himself powerless, a man of death, ever fragmented, unhappy in his self-awareness. This gulf is only bridged by absolute hope, by the anticipation of a fulfilment which is no longer his own achievement; by hope of an absolute future offered as real and possible, a future we call God and which we first really know only in this hope.

The free decision to adopt such hope implies, however, the sort of courage discussed here. In the light of this courage the totality of human existence is hoped for as bringing joy; the basis for this hope is no empirical detail which might be inspected or taken away; this hope is built on God, who is the inconceivable God, the free God. Man must therefore put his trust in another freedom, not a threatening but a saving one. Beyond this hope there is in fact nothing which offers safety or a sure foothold, because the source of the hope, God himself, is only experienced in that hope. And so hope such as this needs courage.

IV Courage as faith

One more important point remains to be made, before I go on to show that this hoping courage is faith in the truly theological sense. It is possible to verbalize and objectivize the nature, content and basis of this hoping courage, as I have done and as all religions do in their various formulations, and deduce from this verbalized reality a free act of courageous hope. It is possible to attempt explicitly to find hope in courage in an explicitly religious act. But however good such an act may be, when the conditions are right, it is simply not what we mean by courageous hope in this sense. For it is first of all far from certain whether, in the contemplative consciousness of man, such an explicit religious act springs from the heart and soul of the person taking part, for only then is the totality of human existence put at risk and so into the hands of the final mystery, God, who saves and reconciles. A religious act, however clear and well-meant, rarely embraces the whole of existence in a valid way. Even if a person says honestly, 'God, I hope in you, I love you', it is by no means certain that what is thought and said is really taking effect, that the person's whole being is moving in a free decision from its innermost centre towards God.

It is even more important to point out how such hoping courage can be seen unconsciously and spontaneously in many different activities in life, where its essential nature is not put in a religious context explicitly and verbally: if someone keeps faith with his conscience right to the end, even when it is not rewarded; if someone succeeds in achieving a love so unselfish that it is truly no longer a matter of mere reciprocation or a bond of egoisms; if someone goes forward calmly and unprotestingly into the night of death; if in his one and only life on earth someone makes his choice unwaveringly for light and goodness in spite of all adverse experiences and disappointments; and if someone — perhaps in an apparently total state of hopelessness and despair — still hopes for hope, hopes against all hope (for hope itself cannot be established for certain as a definite fact, from which further reliable deductions can be made; hope has to be hoped for). In all these instances courageous hope is the motive force, even if it is not expressed in explicit or religious terms. Man's freedom is seen as identical with the hope which is at the heart of human existence and which constantly offers its support to man's freedom through all life's vicissitudes. It is this hope which, unconscious as it is, often gives a person the experience and knowledge of what is meant by 'God', even if the word itself does not normally find a place in such a person's daily vocabulary.

Most of the examples of this free hope in courage are spread fairly anonymously throughout the history of man's freedom. This does not, however, mean that such explicit demonstrations of courageous hope, expressed in religious terms, are in any way superfluous or worthless. On the contrary, they may initiate a full dawning of awareness in the midst of this anonymous hope. So there is a fundamental hope seen in practice at the very centre of life. Moreover such examples protect man where practicable from the danger of losing heart at crucial moments in his history of gloom and threatening despair and from failing in the last act of hope.

This hope full of courage is, however, already faith in the truly theological sense. Many theologians will readily grant this hoping courage the character of 'devoutness', as a sort of human, rather than divine, preliminary form of full true faith, but hesitate to call this hope full of courage 'faith', revealed faith. They would say that this courage of a hope without reservations, vital though it is for man's existence, ought not to be called faith, because faith in the strict theological meaning of the word is a positive affirmation of God's personal revelation and this is not present in the case of man's hope, when it does not come 'from above' and so therefore cannot be described as 'believing'.

A 'lay' theologian, on the other hand, will perhaps be too swiftly inclined to view this hope as the saving faith, feeling that a man who seeks God in hope must certainly find him. That may well be the case, but it does not go far towards answering the question put by a theologian who maintains that a genuine belief in revelation is necessary to salvation, as testified both in Scripture and in Christian tradition. He cannot see his way to recognizing how this hope, this absolute courage, can be faith's answer to God, as he reveals himself at a personal level.

It is, however, perfectly possible to maintain (and the apparent naivety of the layman is thus justified) that such hope is revealed faith, even if only in a rudimentary form that will develop its full nature later. How? First of all, we should reflect that freedom is always the acceptance in a free decision of what lies hidden in the unconscious. Freedom is always the acceptance of a 'risk'; it is the ability to dare further than the explicit and conscious goal. This is especially true of the act of hope in courage, with which we are concerned here. For here the sum total of man's existence, inadequate as it is, comes face to face with the incomprehensibility and freedom of God. Everything is hoped for, the ultimate, even God himself, in an effort which overcomes all individual obstacles and private encumbrances which burden a man on his way through his own history. It is not a question of hoping for more and more, ever new, trivia. The hope is for God himself. It is hope that the movement of the spirit in freedom, over each and every person that can be touched by it, will not finally go astray into the void or come in the end to a halt at one aspect of life which seems the only possible fulfilment, some 'earthly' good. It is hope that the impetus will take us to God himself, the original fulness and the creative source of all aspects of life. God himself is the absolute future of our hope. This is not simply our own natural potential, but a gift that could be denied us, it is grace itself. God himself is the dynamic heart of this unrestricted movement of hope towards him.

In making himself the dynamism and the goal of our hope in his grace, God is truly revealed to us. Grace, which is given to the spirit, the possibility of hope granted by that grace, which reaches out towards that goal, God himself, is truly revelation. It does not need to be consciously understood as such, nor to be distinguished consciously from all the other experiences of a man who is spiritually free, nor even to be explicitly recognized as different by the individual concerned. Nothing alters the fact that it is a truly personal and divine revelation. It does not, in this instance, result directly from the communication of certain dogmas, but springs from the heart and soul of the free person, breaks open this heart through its dynamism and exposes it directly to God and so gives it the courage to hope for everything, that is, to hope for God himself. This inner spiritual dynamism of man should be accepted and not retarded and reduced by any false modesty (implying a last secret fear of life), so that no other good is sought as the final goal of life. If it is accepted, then what we call faith, in theological terms, is already present.

This acceptance of unrestricted and unconditional hope in freedom must not initially be considered as an explicitly religious occurrence. Whenever a man is true to the dictates of his conscience, whenever he does not reject an unconditional hope in the final moment of decision in spite of all disappointments and disasters in his experience of life, that is revelation. That is faith. In Christian terminology, that is the work of the Holy Spirit, no matter whether it is put explicitly into words or not. The acceptance of life in courage and hope sets a person free into the saving and incomprehensible greatness of God and his freedom. It can take place in the midst of the dull everyday life of the ordinary man, because even this everyday average man cannot avoid such ultimate decisions, even when they seem usually to be very unobtrusive. Faith of this sort can therefore flourish in courageous unconditional hope, where religion as such is scarcely or not at all formalized. This faith can even flourish where a man, for whatever reasons, draws back from giving a name to what is inconceivable and so nameless in his life. Hope in courage, which is what true faith is, is in demand everywhere and is found everywhere, even among those who are only anonymous Christians. True faith in the full sense of the word is only possible in free hope, which is absolute courage; and such absolute courage in unconditional hope is, conversely, faith in a real Christian sense.

V Courage as Christian faith

This courage of hope, faith itself, can also be considered from an entirely different viewpoint, that of the courage needed to acknowledge an explicitly Christian faith, to hope with an explicitly Christian hope. The impression has perhaps been given by what has been said so far that, because of the almost incalculably large number of doctrines and dogmas in all the branches of the Christian churches — in spite of confessional differences of opinion — the Christian faith of the Church is something quite different from the faith in hope which we have been considering. It might be thought that the courage required for the acceptance in hope of the total sum of man's existence is something quite different, more simple and natural, than the courage the believer needs to cope with the complicated doctrinal structure of Christianity and its detailed theology.

Certainly the courage required is not identical. Everyday common sense, as well as long-held Christian conviction, both provide us with instances where a person has that deep faith in courageous hope and turns his whole life towards God. He carries out his faith freely in the plain everyday terms of love and duty and yet quite blamelessly cannot find the courage which is an essential requirement for a Christian's belief vis-à-vis the whole body of Christian teaching. Man's present situation in life is one in which he lives in the midst of an intractable tangle of religious and secular opinions. It is therefore understandable that, in the face of the intellectual difficulties involved in understanding a subtly formulated and almost superhumanly articulated Christian faith, a man should give up the attempt through no real fault of his own and adopt an indifferent and sceptical attitude towards Christian doctrine. This is already happening widely among the educated and non-educated alike. Nonetheless it must be said that basically the courage needed for Christian faith is in fact nothing other than courageous hope in a concrete non-abstract form. So ultimately the same courage is required and the two easily recognizable forms in which it appears are distinct from one another in the way that a grain of seed and a flower that blossoms later are different.

To see more clearly how this is so, we have to look at what the Christian faith teaches in its message and find out what is at the heart of the message.

Firstly, Christianity does tell us quite explicitly about what we have described as the 'content' of faith lived in hope and courage. It tells us that we may hope that all vanity, darkness and death will not have the last word, that we may hope absolutely and unreservedly, that we may hope for God himself and know him in the boundless and unconditional nature of his love. It tells us that we may, indeed must, have the courage to go on hoping, even when we have just rejected this hope despairingly in what we as Christians call guilt and sin. It tells us that we must let ourselves be forgiven in this hope, precisely when it seems to us that our guilt is hopeless and insuperable. This courage, inspired by God himself, breaks through the banality of our everyday life and the tired scepticism of our spirit. It is a difficult courage, which demands the last strength of our heart and will – a strength that is no longer our own. But in this respect the courage needed for hope in our life and the courage needed for Christian faith are in the end the same. It may certainly also be true that the religious expressiveness of this hoping courage in Christianity, compared with the anonymous faith in the secular world outside Christianity, not only inspires and promotes the anonymous courage for life, which in its absolute form is faith itself, but presents it with a new problem, just as a conscious theory of action often makes it difficult for the action to be carried out spontaneously and intuitively.

Secondly, as well as the message that both sorts of courage in faith are in fact the same and are only different, as spontaneous and conscious patterns of life are different, there is another fundamental message in Christianity: that of Jesus Christ. What has this message to tell us about the crucified and risen Jesus? Only that in this man, destined to die on the cross, absolute hope is triumphant and reaches its goal; that the perfection of hope which is ours has become tangible and historical for us, when we recognize Jesus' resurrection in faith; and that the perfection of our hopes, the centre of our existence, has been given God's irrevocable and historical approval. There is no space here to illustrate how what I have just said about Jesus is an integral part of the classic orthodox Christology of all the Christian Churches. That would naturally require a more detailed examination than is possible here.

If we start, however, from the thesis as it is presented here, then the situation of the believing Christian today, his courage in faith, is relatively easy to present, and is certainly in accord with the dogmatic conscience of the average Christian and non-professional theologian. The modern Christian experiences Jesus, crucified and

risen, who falls into the total powerlessness of death
and is yet saved and, once saved, is experienced and
known in the faith of his disciples and of all Christianity. He comprehends Jesus therefore as an historical
forerunner, as doing what he himself hopes in courage
to do, what I have already described as the final act of
our existence.

Final courage for life and explicitly Christian faith in
Jesus, crucified and risen, are not therefore two different
areas of the one Christian belief, which are then put
together.

Christian faith, fulfilled and successful in Jesus,
granted us by God, provides what a Christian, indeed
everyone, hopes for himself if he accepts his own life in
hope, even when confronted with God's incomprehensibility and his own death. In spite of the the very
necessary theoretical distinctions drawn between the
ultimate courage for life and the systematic faith in Jesus
Christ, these two are ultimately one and the same for
a Christian. They forge a relationship which influences a
Christian. He believes in his own 'resurrection', that he
will be saved when he dies, and so he believes in the
resurrection of Jesus, which is no longer just an historical
event for him, but a realization of his hopes for his own
life. Because of his own humanity, he gives his believing,
hoping assent to the crucified and risen son of man, in
Jesus. But the converse is also true. Not alone, but in
company with Jesus' disciples and Christians throughout history, he finds the courage of his faith that Jesus,
when he died, did not depart into empty nothingness
but straight into the saving freedom of God. That is
what gives him the courage to confess his own hope, as
he experiences it in his life, and keeps him from ever
resigning himself to a final culpable despair. Because he
believes in the *God*-man, he has the courage and hope to
believe in himself and in the highest possibility, being
with God.

There are, of course, many references throughout the Christian faith to its central vital message and to the process of living in courage and hope, which is so much a part of it. In particular, Jesus' bond of communion with us is stressed, Jesus, the historically tangible revelation of God himself. There are also references to the Church, to the sacraments as the concrete signs of the Church in the life of the individual Christian, to Christian life, to Christian moral teaching. But all these references to dogmatic and moral theology have only one source: they all are derived from this ultimate faith in the Risen Jesus. For a Christian, faith in Jesus is his courage in life translated into real terms in which faith, hope and love are all one. From this point the developments of the Christian faith are too many and varied to deal with here.

It may well be that the individual Christian finds that such derivations and references to specific articles of faith are of little relevance to his real life or to his faith in Jesus, the risen Lord, or to his courage for living. He has no need to refute individual articles of belief, nor has he the right nor the duty to do so in the face of what Christians in general believe. He should let the matter drop temporarily and trust to the further development of his own living faith within the faith of the Church, keeping an open mind and heart.

It is far from certain that we have been given a last and total courage for life to ensure us a more successful existence. For this courage is our freedom acting upon our life. But the individual can reject this action in his life, whether he deals soberly or energetically with the thousand details or tasks he has to do. But if the courage for total hope for success in life is given, then it is grace given by God and has its source in the immeasurable freedom of God himself. Courage and hope bring with them faith, truly present in the Christian sense and brought to its fulfilment in freedom. When, however, an individual gives a positive answer, endorsing his ultimate courage for life, to the question which his courage asks him in hope, as he looks at Jesus, crucified and risen from the dead, alive in history, then Christian faith is present in its explicit and genuine form. This human expressly Christian courage comes from unconditional hope and is difficult and easy at one and the same time.

Translated by Rosaleen Ockenden

PART TWO: FREEDOM AND MANIPULATION IN SOCIETY AND THE CHURCH

Foreword

This section consists of a lecture to the Catholic Academy of Bavaria on 'Freedom and Manipulation in the Church' and a paper given originally to a university gathering in Paderborn on 'Freedom and Manipulation in Society'. Since these two papers to some extent overlap and are also mutually complementary, I feel that it is permissible to present them as a single text.

The lecture was given in Munich on the occasion of the founding of the Guardini Prize by the Catholic Academy in Bavaria and its presentation to me. I would like to express my sincere thanks to the Catholic Academy in Bavaria in this book for having bestowed the prize on me. The theme that I shall discuss here is certainly neither new nor original. It is, however, of great contemporary interests and for this reason always worth while thinking about again and again.

Before dealing directly with the theme itself, it is important to make a preliminary remark. The subject that we have to consider belongs first and foremost to the sphere of the political and social sciences and possibly also forms part of a philosophical study of man as a social being. The more concretely a theme belongs to this field of study (and manipulation obviously points in the direction of concrete realities), the more clearly can it be seen that only a sociologist is really competent to investigate it. I am not a sociologist and I do not even have the sociologist's battery of concepts at my command. I cannot therefore claim to be competent to deal with the theme as a sociologist.

All the same, I have often been struck by the fact that 'manipulation' is not a real key-word in modern dictionaries of the political and social sciences. The non-specialist does not therefore necessarily have to feel that he is excluded from a discussion of this concept. A theologian, then, may be permitted to say something about this theme and, what is more, as a theologian and not simply as an amateur in the field of sociology. His self-justification here is that he cannot regard his own theology of itself as a science with regional frontiers, since, even if it is seen in a very narrowly defined light, theology is concerned with man as a whole and in all his aspects. A theologian can also justify this use of the theme of manipulation to the social scientist by being able to provide, from the storehouse of his own theology, reflections and possibly even deep insights that may be of interest to a sociologist. It is not really possible to know whether this *a posteriori* justification of a theological reflection about manipulation will convince sociologists until the reflection itself has produced some effects. In the meantime, I am bound to stress that this paper is above all theological and not sociological and to this I would add that the theological considerations contained in it are fragmentary and chosen rather arbitrarily.

In what follows, I shall first make a number of observations about the concepts mentioned in the title of this essay — freedom and manipulation. Then I shall go on to say something about the relationship between these two concepts, in order to throw light on the concrete problem with which we are concerned in this paper —

freedom and manipulation in society and the Church. Finally, I will draw a number of conclusions from my theological reflections about the two concepts and their relationship with each other.

I The concept
of freedom

Let us first consider the concept of freedom. It is really rather suprising how unquestioningly those who are fighting today for more freedom in society in general and in the Church use the word freedom, both in speech and in writing. It is not as easy as many freedom-fighters believe to say what is really meant by this word. It is certainly not clear what responsible freedom of choice is in the psychological sense and how it can be justified and verified. Nor is it clear how it is related to social freedom and why the latter ultimately cannot be thought of without the former, although they are not identical. It is also not clear how and why freedom (both in the latter and in the former sense) can, if it should be itself and not be emancipated from its involvement in a certain specific content, which should be itself. No, freedom is for something and this point of reference, the object of free action, decides whether this freedom is good or bad and whether it really should be or not. It is not clear too how and why this freedom does not at that moment simply lose its rights with regard to other freedoms and powers by choosing what is morally bad and should not be.

A theologian ought to point out in advance that, on

close inspection, both the concept and the reality of freedom again and again escape from reflection into the sphere of incomprehensibility, where man and God ultimately dwell. In making this affirmation, a theologian is therefore bound to warn himself and others that this affirmation can be so misunderstood that freedom may be subject to such mystification that it may not be worth fighting for in the concrete or that it may not even be possible to fight for it.

To affirm that freedom is a mystery does not mean that it is not necessary to fight for the concrete possibilities of such a freedom in society and the Church. It does, however, constitute a fundamental warning of the danger of exchanging freedom for something else or regarding something else as freedom or a greater space for freedom, simply because it eliminates an earlier compulsion or a previously existing restriction on the space for freedom.

I should like to begin by reviewing briefly a number of theological theses about freedom. My choice is rather arbitrary. The first is freedom in the strictly theological sense. In the New Testament, this freedom is orientated towards God through the Pneuma in Jesus Christ. It is freedom with regard to the powers of enslavement formed by sin, death and radical selfishness which prevents man from loving God and his neighbour. There is also freedom in the social sense (this exists both in secular society and in the Church as a social reality). Both these freedoms are interconnected.

This is not the time and place to discuss in greater detail the essence and existential reality of this religious freedom or to show that it is not an ideology that has no meaning for man. I cannot enlarge on why it is not a projection of a social freedom into the other world beyond the real world, a projection of a freedom that can only be acquired here and now so that the mythology of religious freedom is made superfluous.

I feel bound, however, to say this. The idea that man, as a Christian or as the philosophical subject of freedom, is still free, even when he is born in chains, is extremely dubious and may be fundamentally wrong. This is clear from the fact that one man can deprive another man by murder (of his biological or psychological reality as a human being) of the possibility of freedom, even in the theological sense. It is possible to dispute this and argue that no man can completely deprive another of every possibility of expressing his religious freedom, because the other can always have an attitude of freedom towards such an attempt. Even if this is asserted, it cannot be denied that there is an essential relationship between religious and social freedom as the conditioning factor of the possibility of the former.

The freedom of the religious subject of love for God and fellow men, that is, of the subject of salvation, requires room — spatial and temporal — for freedom within society. The size, content and structure of this space may vary greatly. It is also historically conditioned and, as I shall show in greater detail later on, it can be to a great extent manipulated. This makes no difference to the basic fact that our freedom as creatures, even in the religious and theological sense, can only be expressed in the world, in history and therefore also in society. This means, then, that social freedom and any change that may take place in it are relevant to the freedom that is proclaimed by Christianity as the factor that sets man free and orientates him towards God.

In its original proclamation, Christianity had social freedom as a factor that might condition the possibility of religious freedom very little in view in the static world of the past, in which society was hardly open to change. It assumed rather that the profane space for social freedom was limited by its very nature and was simply a datum that could not be changed, even though it was known as a sphere of religious freedom. Despite this restriction, however, we may unhesitatingly affirm that Christianity is and always has been deeply concerned with social freedom. What is even more important, this question has now become a matter of great contemporary concern in Christian practice, at a time when this space for freedom in the social sense can be changed by man by means of planned action and not simply as the result of slow, passive and unplanned development. If freedom is really the central content of the Christian message of the New Testament, then social freedom also belongs fundamentally to this message and especially now.

Although we can trace social freedom back to the Christian message of religious freedom from 'principalities and powers', I would not claim that this is the only possible basis for the reality and dignity of social freedom. I would not deny that there is a certain civil freedom that can be taken for granted as a profane reality, especially in view of the fact that a real and to some extent verifiable understanding of religious freedom is fundamentally conditioned, now perhaps for the first time, by an experience of social freedom. This is, of course, because all religious concepts presuppose profane ideas as the factors that condition their possibility, even if the religious concepts are not simply mythological cyphers for profane ideas.

Social freedom as such also has its own dignity and right to exist in this mutual relationship of reciprocal conditioning between religious and civil freedom as well as in the space of social freedom. It does not derive its dignity and right simply from what is fulfilled by it or from the fact that this fulfilment would otherwise be achieved less effectively in the practical sense (an example of this is that the desired variety of consumer goods can be achieved more easily in a free market economy than in a planned economy imposed by force).

This social freedom should be itself even when the situation is the same or even better (the 'situation' being what is made objective by it) without that freedom. This comes about (at least in a theological justification) as the result of the fact that man as a theological being is either a subject of freedom in his salvation or else he is not and that freedom is not only a process by means of which a result is achieved (it would, in other words, have been differently achieved in different circumstances), but is also that result itself.

The principle of the dignity of freedom as such can also be applied to social freedom to the extent that social freedom conditions the possibility of religious freedom. First, the subject of religious freedom can only express himself freely, responsibly and definitively in this material world. Second, eternity (as salvation or its absence) is not something that is quite different, situated behind this life in time and space, but is rather something definitive, the end (and transformation) of our real history here on earth. If these two assumptions are correct, the subject of religious freedom is bound to be concerned with the material world in which he expresses and fulfils himself. He cannot be indifferent to the extent of the space offered to him for his religious and secular freedom. The profane reality within which the subject of freedom expresses himself as a subject of religious salvation is not simply the 'opportunity' and the temporary rôle in which he as an actor proves his value and then gives it up for another part. It is far more than that — it is what really enters into the definitive life of the subject of freedom. If salvation is the definitive fulfilment of our present concrete life, the subject of that salvation cannot be indifferent to the concrete possibilities of living that are offered to him. Those that are offered are aspects of his definitive fulfilment in eternity. Those that are denied to him remained denied for ever.

I cannot go into this question more deeply here, but am bound to stress that we should not be crushed by the inexpressible weight of this insight and allow ourselves to think that the 'possession' of God through the beatific vision may replace all such losses caused by being denied a suitable framework within which we can express our freedom. The actual way of directly possessing God is determined by the actuality of our life on earth. To this extent, then, religious freedom is undoubtedly conditioned by social freedom and its space. The fact that theologians reflected very little about this question in earlier periods of the Church's history is not because of the question itself, but rather because they were conditioned by the apparently unchangeable aspect of the individual's concrete position with regard to freedom and the similarly apparent impossibility of any planned change being effected by society itself. (This situation has in the meantime come to apply less and less).

I must now turn to the concept of manipulation. Man's freedom as a creature is finite. This means that, if it is to be itself and to be able to express itself, it must of necessity have a specific finite material and an inward and outward, individual and collective situation which will be historically conditioned and contingent. Freedom that is in itself infinite is always expressed in a finite space and always experiences its 'divine' and creaturely state in that space. This contingent finiteness of the space for freedom is already given by realities and circumstances that exist in advance of the freedom of all men and by the laws of physics and biology. It is also provided by physiological and psychological laws in man, even if these may be to some extent the object of a changing pattern of human behaviour regarding freedom.

This originally defined finiteness of the space for freedom in man cannot be called a manipulation of freedom. When, however, this concrete definite aspect of the space for freedom available to the individual or society is at the same time the object of others' freedom, then it can and must be called a manipulation of freedom. An act of freedom on the part of one individual which, intentionally or unintentionally, changes another's space for freedom before he gives his consent can also be called 'violence' or even 'manipulation' in the metaphysical and anthropological sense and in the theological sense. Both of these concepts — violence and manipulation — can and must be understood in this context in a morally neutral sense, since it is possible for one man's act of freedom to change another's space for freedom by restricting in advance the other's consent and for that act to be inevitably — and therefore not necessarily — immoral. It is, of course, possible to understand the free change, caused by manipulation, in the other's space for freedom before obtaining his consent as either at all times or else in a given situation as immoral and therefore as directed against the other's freedom.

We can, on the other hand, maintain that not every freely brought about change in another's space for freedom before obtaining his consent is as such immoral and at the same time believe that such a change or restriction without the other's prior consent may be immoral. In that case, we are bound to consider what criteria can be applied in order to distinguish between these two possibilities. It is, however, not possible for me to go into this question at the moment. It is more important to consider at this point the neutral concept of manipulation.

In the first place, seen from the theological point of view, it is inevitable that there should be a manipulation of one person's freedom by another. Freedom, as I have said, should be and is also always exercised in time and space and within society. It is therefore simply inevitable that its expression by one person changes another's space for freedom. This expression simply cannot take place if it has to depend in every case on the other's prior consent. There is in freedom itself an aspect of violent manipulation of others and this is already present in freedom and anticipates the question as to whether this aspect of violent manipulation of one person's freedom by another's freedom is, under certain conditions, morally justified or not in concrete cases. Manipulation of the other is, intentionally or unintentionally, a part of freedom itself, and the question as to whether it is intentional or not is relatively secondary.

Manipulation becomes institutionalized in society whenever the definite aspect of the space for freedom of the members of a society is made more general and permanent by the freedom of the individual members of that society or has been made so by them at an earlier period. This can take place in many different ways. It can come about as the result of general patterns of thought or behaviour, the objectivizations of an earlier freedom (it is, in other words, the result of a habit or a historically conditioned social ethos). It can also be the result of human laws (these can, of course, be arranged differently). Finally, it can also take place through the establishment of simple physical, biological, technical and other realities, involving all members of society in sympathy. It goes without question that these different ways of institutionalizing manipulation in society are interdependent and that for that reason man is inevitably manipulated.

From the theological point of view, this manipulation (and especially socially institutionalized manipulation) may be and very often is sinful, above all if it is not seen to be objectively sinful because it is institutionalized or if consciousness of its sinful nature forms the first stage in a legitimate struggle against manipulation that has to be carried out against men who aim to preserve a consciousness of 'innocence' with regard to this institutionalized manipulation, because of idleness, selfishness, the desire for power and so on. This sinful attitude of institutionalized manipulation is often, as we shall see later on, present in the Church.

This sinful institutionalized manipulation quite obviously cannot be adequately eliminated by moral reflection about morally neutral or even good manipulation of the individual or society. From the theological point of view, moreover, it is clearly an aspect of man's concupiscence, because the latter cannot exist in the abstract or be limited to man's purely psychological processes. Concupiscence, after all, embraces every aspect of man's freedom, both individually and socially. It is also determined by the freedom of others and is derived from their free guilt. It makes their freedom competitive and even includes a dynamic element that can lead to new, wrong free decisions and guilt.

I have referred to the traditional theological concept of concupiscence since it can certainly be applied to manipulation so long as the manipulation of the human space for freedom is recognized as an aspect of concupiscence. The latter points to the pluralism of the situation of freedom which cannot be adequately integrated by the subject of that freedom. There are two reasons why it is not possible to integrate the material of the free decision adequately into that decision. The first is the existence of conflicting psychological impulses in the subject. The second is the pluralistic nature of the material of freedom itself, that is offered by society over and above the physiologically and psychologically vital element. This material has a concupiscent character, in so far as it resists an adequate integration by the subject of freedom into the decisions made by that subject because of its pluralistic and contradictory nature. We therefore do not live in a situation of concupiscence because of conflicting inner impulses present in the person's otherwise good orientation towards God. We are subject to concupiscence because our spatio-temporal situation in society is characterized by sin to such an extent that it constantly offers impulses which go contrary to a good orientation towards God. As a result of this, we turn again and again towards the enjoyment of an illusory order that has been established and is repeatedly defended by human selfishness and sinfulness.

It is worth considering what the Fathers of the Council of Trent had to say about concupiscence. They believed that a distinction had to be made between the sin of concupiscence and that of the original free decision made against God and one's fellow men, with the result that not simply the same radical pathos of an emphatic denial is required as against the guilt in the centre of the person as the denial of religious freedom. Nevertheless, this situation of concupiscence both in the justified and unjustified manipulation of man should not be regarded as harmless, as though it were neutral in the moral and religious sense. On the contrary, this situation should not be. It should be changed and if possible abolished. Even in a history that is incomplete, it is what must always be in protest against it.

We now have to consider these two concepts not separately, but together. It should be clear from what we have already said that man is a unity, which is never adequately reflected and never really static, of freedom and space for freedom on the one hand and manipulation on the other (this unity also exists in the dimension of man's social being). Quite apart from extreme cases, which we do not need to consider here, man's space for freedom is always not only religious, but social. In other words, not only is he able to accomplish his salvation in an ultimate freedom above himself in the presence of God — he also has, to some extent, a social space for freedom as a possibility for his profane freedom and, with and in this, also for his religious freedom. He is, then, never absolutely free without any manipulation, nor is he ever absolutely manipulated without any possibility of free choice in society at his disposal. This unity of freedom and manipulation, both of which are always already given, is therefore by no means always legitimate in every concrete case. This relationship between freedom and manipulation is not static. It is constantly changing in history. This change is, moreover, not simply something that man suffers. It is, to an increasing extent in history, something that man can achieve and plan for in freedom. Man's freedom thus has a history and this history is increasingly entrusted to freedom itself. In so far as this freedom, which seeks itself, always and of necessity produces spatio-temporal and social objectivizations (even if these are only a liberation from the chains which the other wishes to preserve), this history of freedom is itself always a history of fresh manipulation of others, a change in the space for freedom that is imposed on others unrequested and, according to circumstances, in a kind of compulsory imposition of happiness.

Let us at this point recall that, despite this dialectical tension between freedom and manipulation which cannot be cancelled out and which has a history, freedom is what should be and the situation of concupiscence of manipulation is what has to be overcome asymptotically. If this is so, then the history of man is bound to continue to be a history of freedom struggling against manipulations, most of which disguise themselves as objectivizations and apparent attempts to make freedom possible.

What I have said so far about the relationship between freedom and manipulation does not provide any basis for an unequivocal definition of that relationship, from which it might be possible to aim at an equally unequivocal imperative for a definite, changing redefinition of this concrete relationship. Concrete imperatives for such redefinition and change in this relationship always emerge, as the result of necessary and justifiable theoretical reflection, from concrete decisions and historical actions, both of which possess their own light and their own evidence. The latter cannot, moreover, be adequately communicated from orthopraxis to the theoretical reason and its orthodoxy. This is what constitutes the hard, difficult aspect of any such changing redefinition of the relationship between freedom and manipulation.

It is never possible to aim at this redefinition simply and solely through the theoretical reason or discussion, however important the latter may be. The decision that redefines this relationship has no one particular bearer that can be justified once and for all. It comes about, on the contrary, in a struggle between many bearers, to such an extent indeed, that this struggle, which continues to be entrusted to history, must become more and more humanized, since this very process of humanization is one of the essential aims of this change. This decision, then, is what brings about a change in the relationship between freedom and manipulation and it has no one bearer that is justified once and for all time. In this case, it can only be demonstrated and justified on the one hand by its factual efficiency and on the other hand it can be shown to be illegitimate by the fact that one has the courage to appeal, with the commitment of one's own existence, to God's judgment and in this way to create a social reality which will counter-balance the decision against which a protest is made.

II Freedom and manipulation in society

Now that I have discussed these two concepts of freedom and manipulation and their mutual relationship from the theological point of view, I am in a position to draw a number of conclusions which are relevant to my theme.

A genuine history of freedom takes place in the relationship between freedom and manipulation. This relationship is not static. It is, on the contrary, a relationship which redefines freedom again and again to its own benefit and in this way changes it. This change takes place, then, through freedom in a constant confrontation with nature and various aspects of history that are based on natural conditions and are therefore characterized by a certain necessity. Because of this, the change is essentially a history; in other words, it is the work of freedom which is always seeking itself and is given over completely to itself, able to lose its own definition and be unfaithful to itself.

In this history of the relationship between freedom and manipulation, it is ultimately not a question of a process that can be made intelligible by means of a model of development that takes place under coercion. It is rather a creative history, evoking man's free responsibility.

In this history, nothing happens automatically and there is no inner principle acting as a previously existing guarantee that this history is bound to reach its goal in this world: in other words, that it will inevitably achieve a greater space for freedom that is real and not simply apparent. The promise of hope in the word of God that human history will really be fulfilled in the eschatological kingdom of God does not include any guarantee that the fight for freedom and a greater space for freedom will always and inevitably end in victory *in this world*. Viewed from the point of view of the word of God, it is, after all, quite conceivable that the eschatological kingdom of God will be achieved more through defeats than through victories in human history. This is also true of the political task in human society. The history that we are considering is open to hope and responsibility. That is particularly true of the history of freedom, since this is bound to take place, in the freedom of man as a creature, in objective forms, and is always a history of fresh coercions: in other words, of a disguising of the space for freedom.

This does not necessarily mean that everything always stays the same in the case of freedom and manipulation, and that change but never improvement occurs in their history. That is not the case, because, in any situation which is inevitably always changing, the earlier manipulation of man cannot always remain the same in a later period. It is bound to assume a different and sometimes even more terrible character, depending on the extent to which the change is not really a change, but also an improvement. What was perhaps in the past simply a connexion can be transformed into a chain that can and even should be broken.

Of course Christians are very sceptical about the history of social freedom; to a great extent they lack the revolutionary power of a reliable fight for victory in social freedom. During the past few centuries, the official Church as a whole has lacked any such current of revolutionary struggle for freedom; the predominant attitude has been anxiously conservative. I shall try to show later on how dangerous and ambiguous this conservative attitude is in reluctantly suffering social change rather than courageously giving the lead in the struggle for freedom. First, however, I must point out that it is not simply wrong for Christians to be sceptical about the history of freedom. If manipulation arises from freedom, that history of freedom can never be sure of an absolute victory in this world by means of which man overcomes his alienation from himself as an individual and in society. There is no eschatological fulfilment in history as such that can be planned, projected and expressed. Because it is history, it can always hold surprises which may seem to us today to be almost the end of history itself. Therefore Christians cannot expect history to result in a paradise within the world which is entirely free and without any trace of manipulation. When Christians, in their eschatological hope of the absolute future and the absolute freedom of the children of God, are conscious that this definitive victory has to pass through death (which is inevitable for the individual and the climax of his impotence and situation of being manipulated), they can at least acknowledge an uninterrupted current of hope in the world. In that, they remain to some extent sceptical and are not surprised that history, despite all human planning, leads to an unplanned situation, and repeatedly to coercions and even fatal collapses.

This attitude can, of course, be distinguished from a naive faith in a definitive victory in the battle for freedom against all manipulation in this world, if such a naive faith really exists in practice, and not simply in theory. If this distinction is made, Christians will not think that they are prevented by scepticism from contributing resolutely and actively to this history of the fight for freedom. In the course of history, however, Christians have not very often made that contribution. It has, on the other hand, still to be proved that they are unable to contribute in this way and that they are prevented by their scepticism about history and its hope within this world from taking an active part in the fight. A decision to take part cannot be forced by purely theoretical means. It is made by history itself, which is open and therefore asks Christians whether they will carry on the action that decides the open question in their favour.

Before this decision is made, however, Christians think they are right to be sceptical, since it cannot ultimately be decided unambiguously whether the earlier conservatism arising out of that scepticism was really absolutely wrong, or whether perhaps it was the task allotted particularly to them by the incomprehensible Lord, whose representative even the Church is not, in the history of antagonistic aspects which cannot be controlled exclusively by men.

Christians are also convinced that their scepticism with regard to the history of freedom is justified because they believe that the cause of freedom is positively served by scepticism of this kind. That is because this scepticism is only an aspect, the other side of the Christian hope of eternal life, which is above history and, even though it is the fruit and fulfilment of history, the fulness of God himself. Because of this absolute hope — in other words, this scepticism — Christians believe that they can commit themselves more radically to the fight for freedom in this world, since they can really lose nothing that they really need.

Christians must have a sceptical attitude, but they must also take care that it does not tempt them to adopt a sterile form of conservatism which will lead them to try to preserve the relationship between freedom and manipulation in society that has been inherited from the past. It is hardly necessary to enlarge on the fact that this type of scepticism can and frequently does tempt Christians to be socially and politically conservative. This temptation is fundamentally opposed to the true essence of scepticism. It is not the authentic consequence of it. This scepticism is, after all, based on an absolute hope in the kingdom of God which can only be given by God and not by man. This hope cannot simply be a theorem of Christian ideology. It must be a real action, communicated to the world. This action, however, rejects the type of conservatism that aims to preserve what has been inherited from the past under all circumstances. At the same time, it rejects the revolutionary utopianism which regards the future of the world as absolute, and which is always ready to sacrifice all tradition.

A purely conservative Christian is not in any sense the Christian who hopes for the kingdom of God. He is a person who does not let go of the sparrow in his hand in the hope of catching the dove on the roof. The Christian who lets go of a guaranteed tradition, however, in favour of something that has not yet been realized but is only hoped for is accomplishing in his courageous anticipation in this world of the future that eschatological hope without which he cannot find his salvation. The Christian must want the constant change of the relationship between freedom and manipulation in society and must also work and fight for it, because this action is necessary for the communication of his eschatological hope, so long as the latter is not simply pious ideology.

This action, which accords with Christian behaviour, will, of course, be different from the activity that Paul described as characteristic of those who 'have no hope'. The Christian task of changing the relationship between freedom and manipulation in society must accord with certain aspects of human life. The average conditions governing human activity must always be observed. The dignity of the individual has to be respected; man today must not be exploited in favour of men in the future. It is also important for Christians to be sceptical in their attitude to traditional values and the future in this world. Normally, the Christian should favour evolution rather than revolution, but it is not impossible, according to Christian teaching, for a type of action to be required that would, in sociological terminology, be called revolution and not evolution. According to Pius XI, this possibility must be taken into account, although a sceptical Christian cannot accept that Christianity has to be interpreted as an imperative for permanent revolution. He would reject this idea because the term 'revolution' would lose its meaning.

The Church has generally speaking not been an outstanding champion for freedom in the struggle that has taken place in society over the past centuries for more freedom. Most Christian individuals and organizations and the Church as a whole have viewed the history of freedom with mistrust. The Church has given warnings and has not taken part in this history. That has certainly been the case in recent history, even though it is possible to point to such historical events as the attitude of the Belgian bishops in the question of the emancipation of Belgium from the Netherlands in 1830 and that of the Catholic Daniel O'Connell in the fight for freedom in Ireland. These and similar praiseworthy events are evidence of the fact that the Church is not always on the side of the 'establishment' and not necessarily conservative (in the concrete and historical sense of the word). It is, however, generally believed that the Church has, despite a renewed Christian understanding of the world, been too firmly on the side of the 'establishment' in recent centuries and opposed to freedom. It cannot, on the other hand, be justly claimed that the Church has favoured 'historical ignorance' or that it has 'distorted history'.

As a rather older Christian and theologian with a certain critical attitude towards myself, I can recognize in myself, as a normal product of the Church of the last century or so, and as a person without very much specialized historical knowledge, a tendency to react in a conservative way and to be anxious and suspicious of everything that is new and untried. Nonetheless, despite all the confusion in the world and the Church, the Christian of today has the task of being the bearer of the history of freedom together with the Church. This does not mean that he inevitably becomes uncritical of society and the world. Indeed, human freedom is today threatened in new ways by society and it is even more important for Christians to take a critical distance from the world in their fight for freedom. The actual relationship between legitimate and inevitable manipulation and freedom cannot ever be decided finally and for all time. There are many compulsions in society, which often result from the intrusion of rational science and technology into a world suffering from a population explosion and an inevitable demand for consumer goods, and which cannot be eliminated from the world. Not all manipulations in our society, with its technocracy and its fixation on consumption, are legitimate. Taking part in a struggle against these manipulations does not mean that a Christian will be wrongly identified with secular and indeed sinful society and its structure. It should mean that he stands at a critical distance from it.

This fight for freedom in society may, for the Christian of today and tomorrow, be a task that is required of him in an entirely new sense, because it may be (although it is impossible for anyone to say exactly) that a maximum of freedom (understood in the correct sense) will soon be a minimum condition for the continued existence of society. As the task and aim of society, freedom does not mean that the individual will be able to do arbitrarily and unreflectingly just what he wants to do. On the contrary, it means, in the social sense, protecting individuals and society as a whole from manipulation by anonymous powers and groups in society. It also means people taking part in the social process; therefore the latter must become as visible and as public as possible. Finally, it means that society will be ready to help an individual to enjoy personal (and religious) freedom by providing him with the best possible material for freedom. In the same way, society will also have the task of making this material available so that an individual can make a responsible choice and thus become, in freedom, what he really is to be according to his inner subjectivity.

If freedom is seen in this light, it is quite possible that a very high degree of freedom, as yet unattained, will be the minimum condition for the continued existence of man. This is because mankind is certainly threatened by mass suicide if this freedom is not obtained. An individual cannot, of course, compel the kingdom of God to come into his own existence by suicide. In the same way, he also has the duty to care as long as possible for that life on earth as the history of his eternal fulfilment. In the same way, an individual Christian has no right to stand passively aside when the whole of mankind is threatened with collective suicide because he thinks that the kingdom of God may come as the result of that suicide. On the contrary, the continued histoiy of mankind is undoubtedly the duty of every Christian. It would seem, however, that this is synonymous with a longing for greater freedom in the sense outlined above. In that case, the Christian has a task and a duty to fight for freedom to an extent that has so far not existed, because what was previously an ideal has become a necessity.

It is even possible to say that there can be no controversy about the theoretical principles of the duty to fight against a manipulation that should not be, and for a greater space for freedom. There is considerable doubt, however, whether Christians are really equal to this fight: in numbers, determination and theoretical knowledge. Do Christians really forgo their own individual selfishness and do they try sufficiently to break out of their own narrow social group in order to work together and with others towards a free and just order in society in which the threat to freedom by totalitarian powers is overcome from within and not simply by armed force?

It may be thought that we in the West may have granted the people of the Third World a greater space for freedom when our governments and charitable organizations have sent them aid. But have we really fulfilled our obligation with regard to freedom in the underdeveloped countries, so long as *Populorum progressio* (Paul VI) continues, through our own fault, without effect: the message of a prophet in a desert of indifference and greed for consumer goods? It is simply not possible to come to an actual imperative of political and social relevance on the basis of purely theoretical theological considerations. Practice is a more complete promise and a more inexorable judgment than theory can ever be. How will it be, then, if we fail if we are measured only against theoretical norms?

III Freedom and manipulation in the Church

So far, I have spoken about the freedom and manipulation of men in society. I have also discussed the relationship between these factors. Finally, I have also pointed to the continuous task of giving man more space for freedom within the social history of freedom. All that I have said also applies to the Church, as a society that is, in contrast with all other societies, quite distinctive. Nonetheless, it is also a human society. As such, freedom and manipulation exist within the Church in a dialectical unity. There is also a need to safeguard the space for freedom, to recognize its value and to extend it within the Church.

There is manipulation in the Church. This is inevitable, because the legitimate free activity of one man is a factor that changes and determines the other's space for freedom in the Church as well as in society as a whole. In most cases, it also changes and determines that freedom before the other's consent is obtained. There is also sinful manipulation in the Church, because the Church consists of men, including those who bear office, who are sinners, even though it is also a Church of holiness. We recognize, in hope, this holiness of the Church that can ultimately never depart from God's grace and truth. At the same time, however, this holiness (which is both objective and subjective) is never an empirically ascertainable fact. It can only exist as a hope and as a task which are constantly renewed and which transmit God's grace again and again through our own personal responsibility.

This manipulation in the Church exists gnoseologically both as innocent and as sinful manipulation, in so far as the Church's kerygma and theology consist of a pluralism of truths that cannot be integrated into a single, positive system that is obviously meaningful. It also exists gnoseologically in so far as the kerygma and the theology of the Church are decided by sinful, theological pride, rashness, impatience and hardness.

There is also both legitimate and sinful manipulation in interpersonal communications between members of the Church and in the relationship between the hierarchy and the ordinary people of the Church. This manipulation can be innocently legitimate, since intercommunication in the Church is always a contingent act of one person's freedom, which might in itself have been different, but which always limits the other's space for freedom and which is usually performed without asking the other person previously. Manipulation can also be sinful, since it goes without saying that all members of the Church, whether they occupy a high or a lowly position, and whether they admit it or reflect about it or not, are sinners. This means that communication between members of the Church at different levels (that is, from above to below or from below to above) always bears the stigma of human sinfulness, lack of love, aggression, intolerance and the quest for power. I said that that goes without saying and that has to be stressed, because this human sinfulness decides intercommunication within the Church just as it decides all other aspects of human life. I emphasize this also because it is well-known that those who are in a position of power in the

Church as in society as a whole also find it easier to disguise the sinfulness of their relationships with others in what appears to be toleration, patience or politeness. All this can be used to justify the possession of illegitimate claims to power, especially under the appearance of what goes without saying.

Innocent and sinful manipulation in the Church can also be institutionally objectivized. It is hardly necessary to discuss in detail the fact that everything to do with the Church as an institution determines and limits the space for freedom within the Church and is, at the very least, an innocent manipulation. This is at least not so in those cases that are connected with those institutional aspects of the Church which are *iuris humani*; that is, those cases which are determined by a human decision which is not to the same degree a previous decision of all men. But there is certainly sinful manipulation in the Church as an institution. That is so not only in the sense that what is institutional has in many respects come about as the result of subjective guilt (a hard and unloving attitude, an unjust pressure for uniformity, and so on), but in the sense that certain aspects of this institutional dimension are characterized by sin, without any clear possibility of an adequate separation. To express this more simply, we may say that there are quite possibly laws in the Church which are *iuris humani*, as normal Church practices applied in the government of the Church and as pastoral measures that are universally adopted. These laws may well be as they are because they are the result of human guilt. They may also, however, be sinful in that the human sinfulness of the situation of concupiscence has been both inwardly and outwardly decided in advance.

There is also freedom and room for freedom in dialectical unity with this manipulation. This exists in relation to freedom in a transcendental religious sense and in a religious sociological sense. The first aspect is implied in the conviction that the Church is, by virtue of its teaching, sacrament and *koinonia* of hope and love, the place of that salvation that can only be brought about in religious freedom and is indeed itself the fulfilment of that freedom. The second aspect is present because, according to the same conviction of faith, the Church, as a historical and social reality, is and can only be that place of religious freedom as long as it contains a space of social freedom in which that religious freedom can be communicated.

This dialectical unity between manipulation and freedom in the Church is not, however, a static polarity of two always equal factors. It implies a history of freedom and a task to fight for freedom. Even in the Church it is always necessary to fight again and again for this space for freedom, to define it repeatedly and if possible to enlarge it. This task is also implied in the teaching of the free charismatic gifts which cannot be extinguished by the institution of the Church and cannot be adequately manipulated.

The history of the Church is not in the same sense a history of manipulation and a history of freedom. It cannot and should not be that. It should tend towards an elimination of concupiscent manipulation of the space for freedom possessed by the members of the Church, even if this can only be achieved asymptotically. This, of course, is a task not only of the official Church, but of all members of the Church, who clearly ought to develop to the point of loving freedom where all the eternal laws of the Church become superfluous and they achieve the full freedom of the children of God. The history of the Church ought indeed to be a history of freedom even in the social sphere of the Church, since the Church, as the universal sacrament of religious (in other words, of absolute) freedom, is radically committed to safeguard the social space of freedom in itself, and if possible to extend it. In the Church not manipulation but freedom most of all characterises its being as legitimate *in possessione* and in case of doubt.

It is possible to throw light on what I have just said in two ways. First the Church ought to have a critical function in society in regard to freedom. That is even more important in contemporary society. The Church can only carry out this function under certain conditions. It must always boldly take hold of its own history of freedom. It must also offer productive and convincing examples of how freedom can exist and develop with a society that is increasingly threatened by total technocratic manipulation. Second, man plans his own history and regards it as dependent on his own activity. That secular history has now become, perhaps for the first time, to an extent that was almost unknown in the past, a history of freedom in which man is engaged in a constant struggle against manipulation that may possibly become total. At the same time, the Church can only be itself if it accepts its historical situation. Given these two factors, we are bound to conclude that the secular history of freedom is, at its present point of development, an aspect of the history of the Church, which the latter must accept and fulfil in a form that is in accordance with itself.

That may sound very obvious. But, if we look at ourselves critically and honestly as traditionally formed, ordinary members of the Church and perhaps also as invested with some degree of authority in it, we have to admit that we are basically on the side of law and order, tradition and the official, institutional Church. That is our instinct, however historically conditioned and questionable it may be. What is known as freedom in the Church is something that we instinctively find threatening. We cannot easily justify it. We acknowledge it only if we have to and the confession is forced out of us.

This reaction, which has become almost constitutional

among older Catholics, is soon seen to be wrong, however, when the nature of freedom and manipulation is subjected to closer theologically examination. This attitude is probably relatively modern and it may have come about in the Church as a reaction to the profane history of freedom, because the latter threatened the Church and Christianity in its actual effects on the surface of history — perhaps in an innocent or perhaps in a sinful way, perhaps even in both ways at the same time. If we accept this as a possible historical explanation of the widespread mistrust among Catholics of freedom in the Church and society, we are bound to ask whether that conservative reaction was ever justified or whether it is not one of those tragic and guilty aspects of the Church that have come about in the course of history, without it being possible to exclude acceptance of this attitude, seen in the perspective of the essence of the Church.

Whatever may be the case, it is the practical task — or, to express it in a better and more modest way — one of the important tasks today of the Church to redefine the relationship, both for today and for the future, in the Church between a freedom that should be and a manipulation that is always to some extent inevitable. This task can even be extended by attempting to institutionalise the possibility of redefining this relationship so that there can be more freedom and manipulation can even be made an instrument of that freedom.

IV Freedom and love

I should like, in this final chapter, to illustrate what I have said so far by a number of more or less random examples. Although what has been said has all the obvious attributes of a theological preamble to a serious discussion of the theme of democracy in the Church, I do not intend to deal with this question systematically here. The observations that follow are simply an attempt to give what precedes a more precise form.

If what I have already said has been correctly understood, it should be clear that there is, in the interrelationship between theory and practice, a close relationship between freedom and manipulation in the sphere of knowledge and the Church's teaching and theological functions. When it is expressed, theory is always practice and practice always implies the acceptance of theory. The expression of the Church's teaching therefore also belongs to that sphere in which there is freedom and manipulation. The institution has something to do with the truth. There is a positive connexion because the truth of God's revelation must take place in the sphere of the Church as a community (it is only real in that sphere). There is also a negative connexion because, whether it is inevitable or guilty, the manipulation that takes place when the Church's message is expressed by the teaching office of the Church may violate the relationship between the members of the Church and truth accepted in free obedience to faith (this may come about through one-sidedness, possible immaturity or even error). In the sphere of knowledge of faith and theology, all Christians, both theologians and individual believers, now have some room for freedom so that they can freely decide about the truth with regard to the official teaching of the Church. They have this freedom in a clear and explicit form because of their free and responsible attitude towards faith. They have it in the first place with regard to the Church's dogma, in so far as they cannot be compelled to believe and cannot be punished for not believing by any social pressure from the Church. In the second place, they have this room for freedom with regard to the authentic pronouncements of the Church's teaching office that have not been definitively formulated, in so far as these are provisional and can only be offered by the Church, to the best of its knowledge, as pointers to the individual's conscience, for him to judge them in responsibility and a spirit of truth.

That is the most traditional teaching. It has often been passed over in silence (and indeed often is now in Rome) or at least thrust into the background of the Christian's consciousness of faith and of the relationship between the individual and the Church's teaching office. A place — and indeed a major place — has, however, to be made for this sphere of freedom as a sphere of truth in Christianity and the Church. If this place is not explicitly offered by the Church in its proclamation of its official teaching, the Church's teaching itself will suffer. Truth, which is present only as a socially conditioned phenomenon, does not exist in the sphere in which faith can live in a form that creates salvation, and an over-emphasis on the Church's teaching authority and its pronouncements — when it can clearly seem to be erroneous — can only lead to a widespread rejection of that authority.

It is obvious that it is not yet simply a matter of course to give an important place to this space for freedom because there is a marked degree of opposition to many of the pronouncements of, say, the German bishops on the individual conscience in 'higher circles' of the Church. I speak from experience. It is certainly open to doubt whether every bishop unambiguously supports any attempt to give room for freedom in regard to the Church's teaching.

Within the unity of the Church's confession of faith, there is a justified pluralism of theologies. In this context, I am bound to stress that, in practice, the struggle for recognition of the formal teaching authority of the Church cannot take place by means of a pure, monotonous and repeated assertion (however correct this may be in itself) that there is such a formal teaching authority which Catholics are bound to respect. On the contrary, this struggle can only be conducted if the authority of the Church's witness, which is, of course, the very substance of Christ himself and the Christian faith, is made so vital that it sustains the formal authority of the teaching office. This must happen to such an extent that the formal teaching authority (however important it may undoubtedly be) appears as a secondary aspect of the whole of the Christian faith and as a part which does not itself sustain, but is instead sustained. It is, however, difficult to avoid the impression that the Vatican and the bishops tend to insist on their formal authority in a number of cases, such as sexual morality and celibacy, in a way that ultimately appears helpless and inefficient, although it is usually accompanied by encouragement. It would surely be better if they would commit themselves actively and positively to the cause so that this gave authenticity to the witness, rather than that the witness gave authenticity to the cause.

We can apply these theoretical considerations to countless cases in the practice of the Church. It has, of course, to be emphasised that this application of theory to concrete practice is never simply a deduction drawn from theoretical principles, in this case, about freedom and manipulation in the Church. What has in fact to be added to these principles is a judgment on actual relationships in the world and the Church and an ultimately irreducible decision of creative freedom, if a maxim for concrete action is to emerge from these principles. Provided that this is explicitly recognised and carried out, several theoretical considerations concerning freedom and manipulation can be legitimately applied to the practice of the Church in the situation in which it is placed today.

We have already said that there should be room for freedom and that freedom should be expressed in the Church. At the same time, it is important not to condemn all free pluralism in the Church that is not explicitly and officially part of the institution as arbitrary and disordered. It cannot be regarded as legitimate to express freedom only when it is positively sanctioned by the official, institutional Church, nor is all uniformity synonymous with order, simply because order can only exist in the Church in a peaceful situation of selfless freedom. With regard to the laws of the Church, we have to a very great extent not yet reached that state of responsible and serene freedom which is protected and justified in moral theology under the headings of being exonerated from positive human laws, *epikeia*, and sometimes even non-acceptance of a law imposed from above by the people of the Church.

A great deal is said nowadays, not always wrongly, about a lack of respect for the Church's laws and authority and about autocratic and arbitrary behaviour within the Church. When these complaints are made, however, it should not be forgotten that these abuses do not come about because of too much freedom and too little manipulation in the Church, but because we have not yet learnt to use our greater freedom responsibly. It is only when individuals learn to use freedom responsibly that a real improvement can be expected. This improvement will not come by returning to the earlier situation in the Church, in which the space for freedom was very small compared with that for manipulation, including what was at that time a legitimate manipulation.

We are now in a position to draw a few conclusions for the practice of the Church from our theoretical considerations. In the first place, the authority of the Church, its pastoral office and *potestas iurisdictionis* must be re-interpreted. There must, of course, be authority, office and power in the Church. There must also be office-bearers, in a sense placed over and against the lay people of the Church and with authority which, in the concrete, individual case (as distinct from total authority as such), is not that of the matter represented in this individual case, but which has a formal character that is distinctive from the matter itself. The necessary task of re-interpreting both office and the rôle of those bearing office in the Church is clearly a continuing process, since it has obviously not yet penetrated fully to the office-bearers themselves. The feudalistic and paternalistic models of office and those invested with office must be broken down and give way to an understanding of office as a function. If it is seen, not in the light of any community, but rather in the light of the Church community as such, this idea of functionality can in fact cover the whole meaning of office in the Church.

This need to re-interpret authority in the Church ought at the same time to warn us that, in a society which has lost its 'father image', it can no longer be normative and efficient to operate with this image in the Church. The modern Christian does not need to summon up the 'childish' feelings of a 'son' for his 'father' with regard to authority in the Church and we would be playing the hypocrite if we were to say that we felt like the 'beloved sons and daughters' of the pope or the bishops. This re-interpretation really means that we should possess this freedom and not the illegitimate manipulation and that the attitude that should prevail in the Church is not that everything is forbidden that has not been explicitly permitted from above. It means too that it should be possible and legitimate for 'basic communities' of priests or lay people to be formed at the grass-roots and for these groups to come about without permission from above. A functional understanding of office in the Church (as distinct from a feudalistic or paternalistic interpretation of office) also implies that a limitation of the time of office is something that emerges almost as a matter of course from the nature of office as a serving function and is something that is in no sense contrary to any office in the Church, even that of the pope.

In passing, it should also be pointed out that certain concrete behavioural patterns ought also to emerge among those holding office in the Church as a result of this new understanding of office as a function. At the same time, however, it is clear that these ways of behaving are not yet fully accepted as a matter of course. Let me given a example of this. The German bishops themselves appointed a number of theologians as members of their consultative Commission on Faith. Nine of these theologians — the great majority, in other words — recently handed a memorandum on celibacy to the Essen bishops' conference, yet, out of a total of more than fifty bishops present, only two reacted with a single line. This is surely a very concrete example of what is meant and, what is more, it shows that it happens when this attitude is not imputed to the individual bishop as such as a moral question. We may therefore conclude that the institutionalized attitude of the bishops is, if I may be permitted to say so, feudalistic, discourteous and paternalistic. This does not apply to the bishop as a concrete individual, who is not in any way struck by this way of behaving. (This makes the matter worse, of course, rather than better.)

Another aspect of this re-interpretation of the Church's office in practice is that official decisions and measures taken by the Church should, as far as possible, be made intelligible and accountable. Lay people do not, in the legal sense, act as judges or as supreme courts with regard to the decisions made by those holding office in the Church. On the other hand, however, office-bearers are certainly in a very authentic and legitimate sense accountable to the Church as a whole, and therefore also to the lay people of the Church, for their actions. In a functional understanding of the Church's office, that office can always be handed on to another through an office-bearers decision (papal nomination or sacramental ordination). It is, however, more intelligible than in a paternalistic understanding of the Church's office if care is taken to appoint someone who is, as far as humanly possible, suitable for the office in question. In addition to suitability, trust plays an important part in a functional interpretation of the Church's office. The person appointed should be sufficiently trusted by the people and this trust cannot, of course, be simply imposed from above. It can therefore only be of benefit to consider possible co-operation on the part of the laity in the appointment of office-bearers, especially as the way of making such appointments in the past has, in this and other respects, seldom provided sufficient guarantee that the person appointed would automatically prove suitable for the function.

Another practical consequence of this new understanding of the Church's office must also be mentioned here. We have already said that the change in the relationship between freedom and manipulation in the Church, which, as we have pointed out, is a continuous task, ought, as far as possible, to be institutionalised. In practice, this means that the Church's office ought itself to give rise to institutions in the Church which run contrary to that office and its dynamism and in a sense form authorities that will act as checks on the office of the Church. It is not necessary to be convinced of the validity of Montesquieu's teaching about the division of power or of the need to apply this to the Church, but it must be obvious that a division of this kind is to be desired.

Let me give three examples of institutions in the secular and religious spheres which point to a need for a division of power in the Church. Firstly, there is a constitutional court of justice in most states and, although this is not entirely independent of the supreme authority of the government in every respect, it is independent to the extent that it does not need to observe certain governmental measures. Secondly, a court of justice itself appoints a counsel to defend the accused whom the court is trying to condemn and the counsel's task is to oppose this intended condemnation. Thirdly, there is even a person in the Holy Office who is independent of the three men appointed as his superiors and accountable only to the pope for checking the legal validity of the measures taken by the Holy Office. Bearing these three examples in mind, it is clear that there should similarly be institutions in the Church with the task of acting as checks and constraints on the Church's office. They should also be counter-authorities, parallel to the office of the Church understood in the usual sense.

I conclude by saying that the relationship between freedom and manipulation in the Church will be subjected to a continuing process of change that will eventually break down the rigidity of traditional attitudes only when certain conditions have been fulfilled. This will happen in the first place when we have a national synod which will, under certain circumstances *(iure humano)* make binding decisions that may even surprise some of the bishops. In the second place, priests' and pastoral workers' conferences must have sufficient independence from the bishops. In other words, it is necessary for the relationship between freedom and manipulation to be understood as an institutional question and not simply as an ideal, a purely theoretical or historical phenomenon or an element of contestation in the Church. If these conditions are satisfied, the calm and simultaneous movement of change in the relationship between freedom and manipulation in the Church will undoubtedly take place, but it should, of course, be remembered that it will never be fully accomplished. It can be institutionalized to some extent, but only asymptotically, since this institutionalization is itself part of history, which is always open and can never be adequately subjected to reflection. A sceptical knowledge that the Church can never, in our present history, be the fulfilled Church of the end of time cannot justify our leaving everything as it always has been. We cannot, in other words, regard the past as more important than the future. The Church is situated within history and this history must not simply be suffered but must be done. It is, moreover, a history of movement between freedom and manipulation. Given this understanding of history, we are able to see that there is a sense of direction that we must learn to comprehend, because it is a movement which goes from manipulation to freedom, the ultimate authority of which is love.

Translated by David Smith

PART THREE: TOLERATION IN THE CHURCH

Foreword

My theme is 'Toleration in the Church'. In theology and ecclesiology the thing intended by this title has not usually been dealt with by that name. 'Toleration' has for several centuries been used as a technical term for a certain desirable relationship between the state and secular society on the one hand and religious conviction and association, religious communities and churches on the other, and for similar relations between these religious groups themselves. The state is supposed to 'tolerate' each of the religious communities within its jurisdiction. Even supposing it has a 'state religion' (itself a matter of controversy), it is supposed tolerantly to accord to all its citizens the same rights of freedom of conscience and freedom of association without discriminating in favour of any of them; the religious communities and churches are required, in their relationships with each other, to respect this attitude of the state and civil society.

Initially (that is in general from the Reformation period), this concept, whose intention was to safeguard liberty of conscience and the right of religious association, nevertheless took it for granted that there would be a religion of the prince, that is, of the state as such, and hence that other religious communities within his territory could expect no more than sufferance, 'toleration'. But from the French Revolution onwards, there emerged into the foreground the concept of the individual's freedom of conscience and association as prior to all such considerations, and of a secular society concerned exclusively with this-worldly goals. Thus controversy about how, in the concrete, to define the rights of freedom of conscience and freedom of religious association could proceed without reference to the concept of toleration.

Within the Church, the traditional teaching on the right relationship between the state and particular religious communities was, until Vatican II, fundamentally involved with the concept of toleration, on the grounds that the true religion, the true Church, could not accord to other religious communities the same objective rights as it was bound to claim for itself from the state as such, and hence that the most it could allow to these others was sufferance, 'toleration'. Vatican II, on the contrary, in its Declaration on Religious Liberty, *Dignitatis humanae*, presents its exposition of freedom of conscience and of religious association without using the concept of toleration. It presupposes, as the given norm in the present-day world, the ideologically neutral state, by which all religious communities, so long as they do not conflict with the secular goals of the state and society, are accorded basically the same rights: rights not derived from the state but from the dignity of the free human being.

Thus even this short history of the concept of toleration shows that for our purpose it must be used with caution, since it did not originally refer to the internal life of any church as such but sprang from another soil. But there is a further ground for caution, of very practical significance. When we speak of toleration in the Church, we are applying the concept to a community with a common 'ideology', shared convictions, a common programme binding on all who wish, by a free decision, to belong to this particular organized community of faith. It is therefore obvious, and must be stressed from the start, that a set of rules, called 'toleration', which belongs to an ideologically pluralist secular society cannot simply be valid for the internal life of the Church. Even if the phrase 'toleration in the Church' is to be used, the term cannot, in this application, simply mean the same as toleration in civil society: though this is not of course to deny that these two essentially different kinds of toleration have something in common, since both concern human beings with a claim to justice, charity and respect for their consciences. Even at the level of organization and structure a community of shared principles and convictions is different in kind from the sort of secular association whose agenda excludes all the ultimate questions of ideological attitude and choice. Even a political party with a programme has different rules for 'tolerant' co-operation between its members from those of a modern secular pluralist state: the party's programme is seen as binding, and a member may in certain circumstances be expelled for serious opposition to it. This cannot in principle be rejected as intolerance. So also with the Church, and indeed more so, since the source of the Church's self-understanding is not simply constituted from below by free association, but precedes all such association; though the decision to join or leave is entrusted to the freely responsible individual, and this not only because of the dignity of the free person but rather because of the nature of the Church's own self-understanding.

We must, then, beware of simply and casually transferring to the Church the norms and emotive associations of secular civil toleration, and condemning all official action towards those who are members of the

Church by their own free choice merely because that action fails to correspond, or only partially corresponds, to the mentality and norms of behaviour of a pluralist and therefore tolerant civil society. A theology of toleration in the Church can certainly not consist simply of adopting the norms of civil society and its grounds for toleration. Such a theology must have its own basis within the nature of the Church itself. This simple observation is a necessary methodological preliminary to our discussion.

Despite the problems attached to transferring the term toleration, with its alien historical origins, to the internal life of the Church, and necessary as it is to give it its own theological basis, there is nevertheless a simple reason and justification for the transfer: the indubitable fact that within the Church, at all times and especially today, there have been questions, difficulties, tasks, struggles and demands which can be broadly covered with the word 'toleration'. Strictly speaking, of course, toleration can only be a term for one among many different ways of overcoming conflict in the Church: this will be made clearer later on. But using this term as a key-word, one can, so to speak, start by taking note of all the conflicts and reforming aspirations evident in the Church, take stock of them, and then ask whether and to what extent the overcoming of such conflicts requires something in the nature of toleration: and then what sort of toleration it would have to be, and with what limits, if it is to be effective in overcoming such conflicts.

The fact that such conflicts do exist and always have existed in the Church is of course a commonplace. The histories of dogma, heresy, Canon Law, relationship between papacy and episcopate, liturgy, even spirituality all testify to this, even if, in accordance with our set theme, we ignore the conflicts between Church and state, and Church and secular society, culture and science. Look only at the last hundred years. Rome versus Sagnier's *Le Sillon* movement; Berlin versus Trier over trade unions and the Catholic working men's associations; battles round the slogans of Modernism, the condemnation of Modernism, 'Reformed Catholicism' and the literature controversy (conflicts of very differing degrees of importance, of course). Slogans like 'Integralism'; struggles between different tendencies in neo-scholastic philosophy and theology, represented even at Rome itself; conflicts around such names as Newman and Erhard; censure or disappropation affecting such men as Humelauer and Lagrange. The last quarter-century has seen 'Humani generis' and its condemnation of *nouvelle théologie*; social-political controversies between Catholics, most recently, conflicts centred on Küng, Kripp, Schupp, the Abbot of St Paul's in Rome, the catechetical group of Florence, Horst Hermann at Münster, and numerous others. We have conflicts between so-called conservatives and progressives; conflicts identified (whether fairly or not) with publications like *Concilium* and *Communio*; conflicts about liturgical reform and priestly celibacy; conflicts on pastoral problems, such as how the Catholic ecumenical movement should proceed over intercommunion and recognition of other churches' ministries; questions of moral theology, especially over concrete norms in the field of human sexuality and pastoral practice towards people married after divorce. At a lower level, within the religious subculture, there is a generation-gap conflict about the life-style of religious orders, between freedom and authority. There are fights over the recognition or rejection of charismatic and pentecostal currents, apparitions and prophecies, forms of devotion and so on. There are controversies of a theoretical or administrative kind, such as 'political theology', 'theology of liberation', or the rôle of the Church in the media. Such an array of slogans, and so many more forgotten or unmentioned. This list is meant merely to provide some

79

mental background and atmosphere for our present discussion, not as any kind of exhaustive enumeration, however summary, of conflicts in the modern Church.

Vatican II recognized that such conflicts not only exist but cannot in principle be avoided, when it described the Church as *ecclesia semper reformanda*. Since it is usually the concrete complexities of such conflicts that determine which is God's side and which the devil's, so that even those that are apparently purely theoretical can usually not be resolved in principle by theoretical reflection alone, it is obvious that individual concrete conflicts are not going to be sorted out and solved in the course of the present discussion; all that will be offered is a few necessarily abstract considerations. Such considerations do not on their own overcome individual conflicts, but they are not superfluous, because it is all too often these very theoretical principles that get damaged or ignored in a particular case of conflict.

In line with the traditional distinction in the Church between the teaching office and the pastoral office, between faith and daily living, we can perhaps group conflicts into those which connect with the Church's faith-consciousness, and hence with the teaching office, and those connected rather with the Church's life of law, liturgy, administration and so on, though the interaction of the two aspects makes the division problematical and difficult to carry through. We shall not lose sight of the theme of toleration in the narrower sense, but it will have to be accepted from the outset that the broader question of overcoming conflict in the Church necessarily breaks the bounds of the toleration theme as such.

I Conflicts

Before I attempt to discuss separately the overcoming of conflicts in the two categories of doctrine and life, there are still some general observations to be made about the ultimate causes of such conflicts and rules for overcoming them which apply regardless of classification.

1. Without making any claim to a clearly-thought-out methodology, I shall begin by trying to say something, at the most general level, about the causes of such conflicts within the Church. My purpose in doing so is to make it clear that they are *unavoidable in principle*, because it is this that brings to light the ultimate essence of toleration, which is precisely the patient endurance of such conflicts.

The ultimate cause of all these conflicts is the unintegrated plurality of human consciousness in the world at large and therefore also in the Church. Every human being's consciousness is finite and limited by genetic, social and individual factors; hence it is inevitably and irremediably different from every other one, no matter how desirably intense the degree of communication between them. This is both the limitation and the dignity of every human being: his unrepeatability. He is never

81

merely the reproduction of a universal idea. Over against the universals 'human being' and 'Christian', a concrete individual is not only non-essential, contingent and corruptible but also unique in his freedom and his own special history; a being of eternal validity and worth. St Paul in his teaching on the multiplicity of charisms in the one Body of Christ is reflecting on this truth; he recognizes that the plurality is given by God and that it is right that it should exist.

No point of reference within history (for example, the supreme leadership of the Church), using some formal system of harmonization-rules, is capable of adequately integrating this plurality of historically conditioned finite human consciousnesses into a unity recognizable as such to us. Rules have to be general; they cannot perfectly fit the concrete reality of each individual consciousness. What is still more important, the authority which is the point of reference for this harmonization has to be perceptible and operative at the human level, which, even allowing for the assistance of the Spirit of the Church himself, means that it has to be one more particular historical reality with its own particular consciousness.

In practice, when the Church is dealing with conflicts between one consciousness and another, this obvious point is often overlooked or repressed. Of course there are such things as decisions, taken by those with full competence to do so, which can and should, in their own way, effect a sort of provisional (in a positive and negative sense) resolution of conflicts, and which are binding on the individual consciousness. But this never achieves a final reduction of plural consciousness to homogeneity; the pluralism remains (this also applies to decisions at the theoretical level). Such decisions do change the situation, but they do not simply eliminate conflicts arising from the plurality of consciousness. This will be made clearer later on when we consider individual conflict-situations. It was necessary at this point merely to point out in general terms this ultimate ground of conflict in the Church, because, as I said before, it is this that points to the very essence of toleration. Toleration does not mean, essentially, an attitude towards some individual with deviationist theories and practice; ultimately, it means patiently and hopefully bearing with the unintegrated and unintegrable historical contingency of a Church which is not yet the perfected Kingdom of reconciliation and unity.

In this matter the Church is like the individual person. An individual human being is caught in the state of concupiscence, intellectual and moral, that is, in a plurality of experiences and opinions, as well as of good and bad impulses, which he cannot completely integrate so long as he is pursuing his own individual history. He must of course strive to approximate more and more to a reconciliation and integration of this state, if his death is to be the point of success at which he receives his final reconciliation from God. An individual has got to accept the 'agony' (to quote the Council of Trent) and determinism of his situation with patience, tolerating and bearing with himself; he must not think that he can prematurely impose an all-embracing system upon his theory of an all-harmonizing model of conduct upon his practice. A similar theoretical and practical concupiscential agony obtains in the Church, only more so, since here we have a multitude of such consciousnesses coming together to form a unity which is always in advance of what can be achieved within the span of history.

A second reason for these conflicts in the Church is the Church's sinfulness. Holy Church always confesses that it is also the sinful Church of sinners, though we cannot at this point go into the question of how the two coexist. The sinfulness affects the Church's decision-makers as well, so that it is liable to set its stamp to some degree at least upon their decisions, even when such decisions are in principle both correct and a legitimate exercise of authority. For they may still be hasty and lacking in love, and be culpably less balanced and less nuanced than it is possible for them to be. It is not of course the case that when conflict-situations are being dealt with sinfulness of this sort is at work only in those who bear office. Egotism, impatience, lack of love, culpable shortsightedness and plenty more kinds of sinfulness are of course just as liable to be present on the other side.

The Church's sinfulness is not merely an empirical fact of human experience but a matter of faith: faith, unlike human complacency, does not repress the fact of the common sinfulness of all human beings but accepts it and the consequences to be drawn from it. Hence allowing for such sinfulness is a specifically Christian task, implying humility and readiness to forgive, and calling, in a heightened sense of the word, for toleration of the sinfulness itself. Donatist impatience, postulating a Church which is *only* holy, with nothing left to tolerate in it, is no proper starting-point for overcoming conflict in the Church.

A third cause of conflict in the Church, closely connected with the first, is that different people's consciousness does not always belong culturally or socially to the same epoch. Though they coexist at the same point of chronological time, they do not necessarily live and act in terms of the same historical situation. The mentalities of particular groups in the Church, though contemporary with each other, are culturally and socially rooted in various different epochs. Hence they inevitably differ from each other, and it is not automatically possible to say that from every point of view one particular mentality (the modern one, for instance) is now the only right and proper one. This disparity of cultural epoch between mentalities within the Church — a Church that is meant to be one and the same

84

Church throughout the world and in all such non-contemporaneous cultures − inevitably creates conflict situations; and since the disparity cannot be removed, the conflicts can only be overcome by toleration, that is, by the full acceptance of the disparity.

Let me add one more supplementary observation. In St Paul's theology of toleration, that is, his teaching about the multiplicity and variety of charisms in a Church which is nevertheless required to be one Church, he stresses that every member does not have every charism. In itself this is merely obvious, but if we really take it seriously it follows that any member of the Church with a particular charism, task − a particular mentality − is going to be unable, in the last analysis, to understand the charism, mission and mentality of some *other* member; there will be a certain irreducible strangeness which cannot be eliminated but only accepted in self-forgetful love and patience, that is, in toleration. You can only really understand what you can appropriate as your own. Hence you can only fully accept the otherness of an individual, a culture or an epoch by dint of a toleration of this alien thing as proper to the Other as such, while remaining unable, in our present unreconciled historical state, to possess it as your own.

Before we can start in more concrete detail on the conflicts within the Church, whether of doctrine or life, and inquire into the tasks and limitations of toleration in the narrower sense, there are some principles to be formulated which apply to all such conflicts and also have something to do with toleration.

2. All conflicts and the overcoming of conflict must be seen and treated in a Christian way. This involves, in the first place, respect for the dignity and freedom of conscience. This is an obvious proposition, given a fresh emphasis by Vatican II as a norm for the Church itself precisely in opposition to a certain false objectivism. It is not of course meant to be a charter for arbitrary and

capricious subjectivism. Every narrow, shortsighted refusal to accept the findings of a thorough investigation is not hereby invited to adorn itself with the titles of 'conscience' and 'freedom'. But this reservation makes no difference to the fact that the individual conscience *is* the final court of appeal, which can neither be eliminated nor overruled. Nor to the fact that a conscience making an objectively false judgment (on a concrete matter) is still to be respected; and that the question whether, in a given case, what we have here is a genuine judgment of conscience (subjectively, at least, not open to correction) or a bit of self-opiniated arbitrary subjectivism must, once again, be left to the individual himself as the final tribunal under God. Freedom of conscience in this sense has got to be respected absolutely, in matters of religion and the relation of the individual to the Church as much as elsewhere. This means that the only permissible means of convincing a human being on a religious matter is argument; it also means that it is not permissible to induce a person to make an external affirmation or to act externally in a way which contradicts a decision of his conscience.

But all of this is only a part of the reality which we are discussing. The freedom of any individual is always embodied, realized in space and time, and thus with a social reference. It requires room to exist, physically and socially. But any one person's freedom has to share this space with the freedoms of all the other persons who need to actualize their freedom in the same area (not that this implies any fixed and rigid boundaries). Thus freedom in this sense is in itself absolute and unconditional, but the scope of its operation is not. Freedom cannot operate without limit in every way anybody likes, because the area is limited and there are other freedoms laying claim to it as well. The appropriation and defence of the available area for one's own freedom is always, unavoidably, the limitation of someone else's, who wants to lay claim to the same area. Supposing that, in a very abstract and basic fashion, we define force as the modification of someone else's area of freedom without the prior consent of the person whose area of freedom is being modified or reduced. Then in this sense force is not necessarily and always an immoral attack on somebody's freedom, but arises from the nature of human freedom itself, from the plurality and spontaneity of subjects within the same area of freedom.

We must also of course include the case in which a number of free persons come together to form a group, a society, a community, freely constituted, and such a group, as a unit, then modifies the area of other people's freedom without their consent.

This very sketchy metaphysic of freedom and force makes clearer a point already briefly made: the legitimate freedom of an individual who wants to belong to the Church cannot include the voicing of every conceivable opinion or the doing of every conceivable action within the Church as such. The appeal to conscience cannot justify an individual in laying claim to such an absolutely unlimited area of freedom. The Church is a community of consciousness with a particular self-understanding and 'programme'. If, in a matter of conviction or conduct, anyone finds himself fundamentally opposed to that self-understanding and programme, he can indeed, so long as he is not also in contradiction with the socially-defined common good of secular society, declare his conviction in that wider society, appealing to his conscience, and act accordingly. What he cannot demand is that he shall display this conviction and the behaviour corresponding to it within the Church as such. The appeal to his conscience does not give him that right. To do so would be an offence against the freedom, within that area of freedom, of those who have by a free collective decision constituted this particular organized community of consciousness and faith. Respect, 'toleration', for the freedom of the individual does indeed require that he be able, without disadvantage to himself as a citizen, to leave such a free community of shared conviction, the judgment of his conscience being in fundamental contradiction with that community. It does not include his remaining in that community, despite the fundamental incompatibility of his conscience with its convictions, and continuing to advocate his own conviction within it.

There is a further precision required for a Catholic understanding of the Church. The decision whether someone has or has not, in theory or practice, clashed with the substance of the Church's faith or the unity necessary for its life does not *simply* rest with the whole of this free community of faith: not in the sense that the community includes no other specific subject competent to take such a decision, over and above the undifferentiated mass of its members. The taking of such decisions belongs, rather, to those who hold office in the Church, with authority to make binding statements of its common faith and to give effective expression to its unity of life. An official decision of this sort can indeed, in an individual case, be mistaken about an individual Christian and what he is thinking and doing (given that it is not a plain case, looking at it from both sides, of contradiction between a defined dogma and the conviction of the person concerned). But as regards the public life of the Church it still has to be respected, and not emptied of meaning by appeals to the effect that it is objectively mistaken, or is not derived from the Church's real faith-consciousness or the real needs of unity; though the individual concerned does always have the right to appeal once more to the Church's authorities on the basis of better information.

To sum up: freedom of conscience, where the substance of the Church's faith and the unity of its life are concerned, does not justify the teaching and doing of anything and everything within the Church. In itself, this is a statement of the obvious, even when the area of freedom of an individual and his conscience is limited thereby, and all societies based on community of thought throughout the world take it as obvious and put it into practice.

Nevertheless, in practice this principle is often threatened. It happens when some particular community possesses a degree of potential power and influence in society as a whole. There is then a temptation to infiltrate and manipulate it; to join it, not in order to use your membership in accordance with the mind of that community, but to alter it fundamentally, and thus take over its power-potential for some quite different programme. Of course in any real, living society there are principles enabling it to change, as part of the historical process, while maintaining its fundamental identity. Hence in any society, including the Church, there may be movements striving for change by appealing to these principles, and these may in practice involve conflict. But when what is being attempted is the infiltration and manipulation of a community, against its own programme and principles of change – a revolution, in fact – then this is essentially an attack on the freedom of those who really constitute that community and its programme. This is immoral, and the community has the right to defend itself 'by force' – meaning expulsion.

'Force' in this sense is not any attack on the freedom of the would-be manipulators; it is not intolerance in any bad sense. Within a community of shared ideas, such as the Church, it is not requisite that everything shall be possible; freedom in the Church does not imply respect for anything and everything which anybody, appealing to his own conscience, declares to be legitimate or worth striving for. Freedom either to belong to the Church or to leave it, on the other hand, must be absolutely respected. The Church has no right to bring any power or force to bear to limit this freedom, though what the theological interpretation should be of the position of a baptized person who has left the Church is another question, which we will leave open. What was formerly the traditional teaching of the Church — that it has legitimately a greater right to use force against a baptized dissident than an unbaptized one — is out of date since Vatican II. The Church must absolutely respect a person's liberty to leave it; it must resort to expulsion only in genuinely unavoidable cases after careful and searching consideration; it is even bound, in Christian love, to help the expelled person so as to mitigate any inevitable consequences of a secular nature (loss of an official position, difficulty in finding an alternative job and so on); but, faced with a dissident, it must take account of its own freedom as a community of shared consciousness, and it can expel members who, in theory or practice, are trying to manipulate and distort it.

Obviously, only the most general principles regarding individual freedom in the Church have been formulated so far. We have had no clarification of when the individual's conscience, which must be respected, does or does not come into fundamental conflict with the common mind of the Church; nor have any principles been formulated about all those conflicts, theoretical and practical, which can and do happen without involving the fundamental unity of the Church. All that will come later, when we are dealing with individual conflicts of doctrine or life.

While still on the subject of general principles for the overcoming of conflict in the Church by toleration, it must be said, secondly, that for all concerned these principles include the claims of the Christian virtues. If, in other words, such conflicts are to be overcome, we must be recognizing and living the Golden Rule of the

Sermon on the Mount. There must be love, unselfishness, humility, readiness to serve. There must be respect for the incommensurable worth of the individual, for his unique charism which can never be completely understood by anyone else. There must be respect for the value and legitimate importance of the past, and for the demands of a future which can never be satisfactorily calculated in advance; and thus recognition that the ultimate decisions lie with the Lord of history, God himself, subject to no human court of appeal.

This is perfectly obvious, yet in relation to the concrete life of the Church it is no meaningless cliché. Of course men must plan, in the Church as elsewhere. Of course rules must be institutionalized which go as far as possible towards making the overcoming of conflict independent of human subjectivity and goodwill. Argument must reach as far as it possibly can, and action must be taken according to transparently just principles: much can and should be done in the Church to ensure that conflicts are dealt with fairly and realistically. It is undeniable that those who hold office in the Church are often allergic to such efforts. They are not unwilling to avoid argumentative and coolly judicial methods of resolving conflicts by appealing to their own higher wisdom and their own consciences; whereas, contrariwise, when anyone else appeals to his conscience they say that his conscience is incorrect and that argument must be objective. Even very recently it is observable that there is a disinclination at Rome to display the processes of argument to outsiders as plainly as to those who are part of the official machine (the *periti* of the Congregation of the Faith, for instance, who were for a time listed in the *Annuario Pontificio*, have recently vanished into anonymity again).

But still, and in spite of all that: in very many cases if not all, conflicts do not get properly solved simply by the laws of logic, realistic argument, and institutionalized rules about how to solve conflicts. Usually, or always, there remains an area in which judgments are approximate and uncertain, conclusive proofs are lacking, unclarity makes it possible for relevant points to be overlooked or their importance under-estimated. This unlit area within the rational process can then provide a hiding-place (though their presence cannot be conclusively demonstrated) for such forms of sinfulness as egotism, short-sightedness, hardness, lack of love, cowardice and so on, on both sides of a conflict. Hence the summons to the Christian virtues of love, humility, understanding, readiness to give way and so on, can never be entirely replaced by cool, relevant argument. It is certainly not right that such necessary argumentation be pushed aside or short-circuited by unctuous speeches on the part of the authorities or emotional over-reaction from the other side, as happens all too often. But nor, equally, can the summons to the Christian virtues, made perhaps with veritably prophetic force, be rendered superfluous by rational argument alone. Even those in authority must not be beyond the reach of an appeal to their consciences, requiring them to show the Christian virtues and thus calling in question both their rational arguments and their invocation of their formal authority.

In this world, before we arrive at the judgment seat of God, there is no tribunal available whose decision can unambiguously and conclusively guarantee that any particular solution to a conflict shall be humanly, objectively and in every respect right, no matter whose side it comes down on. Nevertheless, decisions resolving conflicts do, unavoidably, have to be taken, even though they must always remain, in the last analysis, provisional, waiting upon a final reconciliation in eternity and upon the judgment of God. Out of this emerges a new perception of the ultimate and comprehensive meaning of toleration in the Church. It is not primarily and ultimately a sort of permissiveness on the part of authority in the face of opinions and demands; nor is it mere respect for formal authority on the part of those who remain unconvinced by authority's arguments; it is at bottom the attitude required on both sides in a conflict, by which they endure to the end the impossibility of a fully adequate rational solution in the hope of that ultimate reconciliation which still awaits us.

3. In spite of the fundamental importance of what has been said so far in the way of general rules for overcoming conflict in the Church, it must also be said that modern rational techniques for dealing with conflicts, increasingly developed in secular society, must find their place in the Church as well, and be given much better institutional forms than they have had hitherto. Such a demand does of course involve a Parkinsonian danger of mounting bureaucratization. Nor must we obscure the fact that the episcopal constitution of the Catholic Church places a personal responsibility and authority upon those who bear office which cannot in the last analysis be delegated or transferred to any 'democratic' body. Nor would such a transfer always have the effect of making decisions absolutely rational and transparent, since 'democratic' decision-making also has its limits. Indeed, decisions taken anonymously, behind the scenes, quite often precede and influence those taken in democratic bodies, and these pre-emptive decisions, which are the real ones, and the motives behind them, do not really come up in the open discussions at all.

Nevertheless, it must still be said that sensible, sanely-applied modern techniques for dealing rationally with conflicts have their place in the Church today. For example:

Consultative bodies which really are listened to, and with which the authorities argue rather than laying down the law.

Dialogue.

The right to public debate on matters of conflict.

The right to criticize without having criticism instantly strangled by those in office invoking their supposedly superior information, their divinely guaranteed higher wisdom, and their formal authority.

Maximum flow of information.

Maximum public explanation of the grounds on which a decision has been taken.

Procedural rules for dealing with conflicts at the theoretical and practical levels.

Possibility of appeal to a higher tribunal.

Arbitration courts of various kinds, where appropriate.

Separation of powers, wherever this is, to a significant degree, a possibility for the Church.

Clarity about when, where and by whom the real decisions are made.

Right of access to dossiers, personal files, and so on in ecclesiastical offices.

The right to counsel of one's own choosing when one is the subject of proceedings.

And so forth.

Something, it is true, has been done about all this since Vatican II: this is not the place to go into details. But surely a great deal more could and should happen in this direction. It ought to be possible to hope that the new code of Canon Law will bring about an advance: that such institutionalized means for dealing rationally with conflict will actually be put into practice; that the members of the Church will get to know them, grow accustomed to them, take them for granted; and that they will not be constantly set aside by summary procedures.

4. In today's situation a fourth thing has to be said, more explicitly than hitherto, against those in the Church who think that so long as freedom is respected, dialogue willingly maintained, negotiations not broken off, everything kept open, all conflicts in the Church can be

resolved without the need to take any decisions which go against the conviction or desire of anyone concerned. This is utopian, and possibly not a very nice Utopia either. Ultimately, it dissolves that pluralism of freedoms in relation to one another which belongs to historical existence and so to the historical Church. It logically involves the denial of any formal authority, which it reduces totally to the authority of the arguments themselves (which is false). It denies that office in the Church derives its powers from the nature of the Church, and hence from the will of Christ, as opposed to being constituted simply by the agreement of the Church's members. It is as impracticable in the Church as in any secular society: here too decisions have to be taken which run counter to the opinion and desires of individuals, and it is no comfort to those thus affected if the decision has been taken, not by an individual, but by a body in which they themselves have directly or indirectly participated. If government (whether exercised by a body or an individual) simply means that there are necessary decisions which run counter to the convictions and desires of some of those whom they affect and are nevertheless binding on them, then government is something necessary and unavoidable in any society. Hence also in the Church. And if there has to be government in holy Church, then there must be such a thing as a holy government, a hierarchy, true though it is, as especially stressed since Vatican II, that this government is required to operate as service and not as autocracy or paternalism. But the fact that there will always be a need to combat these distortions, because anyone who holds power is always under this temptation, does not alter the necessity for government in the Church, in the sense stated, nor the fact that its legitimate exercise may run counter to the convictions and desires of someone affected by it. There do have to be decisions in this sense even in the Church. Once again:

this fact is not in the last analysis made any less tough and painful by the decision-maker's being a body constituted in some democratic way. This can to a certain extent improve the rationality and transparency of the decision, but it cannot in principle remove the possibility of a tough and painful conflict between the final decision and the opinion of someone affected by it.

Once again, this brings into focus the source whence springs toleration within the Church. In origin at least it is one and the same as patience: a Christian quietly and calmly takes account of the fact that he can be affected by decisions which contradict his own opinions and goals, and that within the ongoing history of the Church there can be no simple resolution of this contradiction. For even if he subsequently gives, as he is often required to do, an external and internal assent to the decision, this does not simply and totally resolve the contradiction, but leaves behind a residue of mutual misunderstanding and mutually inflicted wounds.

II Doctrine and authority

And so we come at last, as long promised, to the subject of doctrinal conflicts in the Church and the role to be played in them by toleration on the part of all concerned but especially of the official teaching authorities; though the nature of the subject makes it impossible to deal with toleration of this kind on its own, and it will be necessary rather to consider doctrinal conflicts in more general terms. It is obvious, from considerations of space, that the theme will have to be discussed very selectively. A further justification for restraint is that the subject-matter of the theme has been dealt with for centuries as part of fundamental theology and ecclesiology. It arises in discussion of the teaching authority of pope, councils and bishops; of the grading of these authorities and the binding character of their declarations; of the nature of heresy and orthodoxy; of what theological note, in terms of how binding they are, to attach to which theological propositions; of the extent and limits of the competence of ecclesiastical teaching authorities; of the difference between faith and theology; of the hierarchy of truths within the totality of the Church's proclamation; of the difference, even in the dimension of faith, between the private and public sphere; of the different degrees of personal assent to matters of faith and doctrine proposed by the Church and so on. It must not be thought that the question of toleration in the field of doctrinal conflict has never been dealt with in the Church's theology until our own day. Since that is by no means the case, and since it would be quite impossible here to make a comprehensive and systematic survey of everything involved, it will be right and necessary to confine myself to a few selective observations.

1. First of all, there is something we must be quite clear and firm about: it is part of the self-understanding of the Catholic Church that the substance of the faith is binding in character and constitutive both of the Church itself and of individual membership of it; that it follows from the nature of the Church and the mission of Christ that its proclamation of this message is authoritative; and that when it is offered to the individual, for his free assent, it is objectively, morally binding. It is true that this doctrinally formulated substance of the faith has its roots in something deeper: a living experience of God and Jesus Christ in the Holy Spirit. The doctrinal, propositional formulation of it is nevertheless constitutive. There are and always have been dogmas, absolutely binding statements of faith which, despite their historical conditioning and their particular history, despite differences in value between them, despite their being open, while keeping their identity, to better and more assimilable interpretations and re-formulations at a later date, are constitutive of the Church's faith and of the understanding of that faith by which any individual Christian can be in the full sense a member of the Church.

It is Catholic belief that the Church is not only preserved in God's truth by his Spirit in respect of that deeper ground of its faith referred to above, and in its proclamation of that faith in general, but also in each particular statement, *on those occasions* when it commits itself to them absolutely, as part of its proclamation, and calls for the absolute assent of faith to them, as something revealed by God and thus constitutive of its faith. There are 'infallible' dogmas in this sense, whatever disputes there may be about the intelligibility or assimilability or redundancy of the concept.

There are also, according to Catholic belief, clear and recognizable teaching authorities for making these absolutely binding statements: the teaching and believing Church as a whole, realizing and expressing itself in the ordinary proclamation of the message by the episcopate as a whole with and under the pope; and the more reflectively reconsidered affirmation of that ordinary teaching in solemn definitions of councils and popes.

Whenever an individual Christian contradicts a dogma of this kind head-on, not merely in the sense of expressing an opinion but as an ultimate, personal decision, formally equivalent to the decision of faith, he ceases to be, in the full sense, a member of the Roman Catholic Church; at least if his 'obstinate' conviction impinges upon the public life of the Church and its shared faith, he becomes in the old-fashioned sense a heretic or even an apostate. In such a case the Church has the right, even sometimes the duty, to make this person's self-separation from the Church and its faith explicit. It has the right to deny him such rights and opportunities for action within the Church as he may still, perhaps, claim for himself. It has the right to take defensive action against 'infiltration' and 'manipulation', even though, in any particular case, such measures may not in fact be successful, and a broader view of the Church must see its defence as ultimately a matter of trust in the protective power of the Spirit, and not in administrative or police measures taken by Church authorities.

2. However clear this formal principle may be, and however necessary it is to stress it against current

tendencies in the Church towards the dissolution of dogma, it is of course the case that many of the more practical questions that arise, even over conflicts about actual dogmas, are very difficult to see through. True, the teaching authority is not merely competent, while appealing to Christ, scripture and dogmatic tradition, to proclaim and teach dogmas as absolutely binding. It is also 'competent concerning its competence': meaning that when the Church proclaims something as dogma revealed by God, the individual member cannot evade the demand thus made upon him by the teaching authority by asserting that the matter in question is not in fact a truth revealed by God, and thus not within the power of the Church to lay down as ultimately binding. But this goes nowhere near solving all the problems classifiable as doctrinal conflicts, even if we confine ourselves to the sphere of actual dogma. Even the proclamation of dogma as such, and hence the perception of the formal authority of the teaching office, run into difficulties today which were not present, or not to the same extent or with the same sharpness, in former times.

What, for instance, is to be the attitude of the teaching authority when a Christian, or a theologian, is *not* simply, decisively, and in his own explicit terms rejecting a dogma of the Church, but is putting forward (perhaps as opinions for discussion) teachings which seem at first sight to contradict some dogma; but which, again, given the distinctions being made today, and to-day's conceptual pluralism, not susceptible of any thorough-going systematization, are not after all so easy to identify as clear, unambiguous contradictions of any dogma? Suppose it is possible to ask whether this suspect teaching involves a contradiction only in a matter of terminology, or only in regard to a misunderstanding of the dogma, or an interpretation of it which, though it has been indiscriminately taken for granted as part of the dogma in the past, and handed down along with it, is now emerging as not identical with it at all? We have today an irreducible theological pluralism: nor is it possible for reflection to be sufficiently precise in distinguishing between a particular theology and a statement of faith as such. Suppose some episcopal or papal teaching authority which is at home only in one of our various theologies is called upon to pass judgment on the statements of a theologian who works with quite different perspectives and terminology? A sound judgment in a case of this sort calls for an expertise in such things (depending on the individual case) as exegesis, history of dogma, philosophy and sociology which cannot be assumed to be present, in any but the vaguest form, in a small body set up to give an episcopal or papal decision on such a matter. And because they do not share his presuppositions, such expertise, even if available, will not carry the same weight for the members of such a body as for the theologian upon whose teaching they are to pass judgment. How do such difficulties look in the case of Indian, Far Eastern or African theology, developed from its own autochthonous non-European milieu? These are the kind of difficulties that arise today. They still arise when the point at issue really is dogma as such, but the interpretation of it by a given theologian is not, on the one hand, in an immediately perceptible way or in his own declared intention a contradiction of that dogma, nor, on the other hand, clearly and certainly compatible with it in its binding sense.

Now, in such cases there is certainly a need for caution, patience, keeping the dialogue open, understanding — in a word, toleration on both sides. First, toleration is required from the official representatives of the teaching Church (note that I am still speaking of cases concerned with the compatibility of a theological opinion with actual dogma). They must, with genuine tolerance, be really clear about the difficulties indicated above in reaching a decision. They need to be clear about their history of dogma. There have been plenty of cases of merely apparent, merely verbal heresy which, given more toleration and breadth of mind, heart and understanding and less patriarchal authoritarianism on the official side, need not have got to the point of splitting the Church (though only schismatically, in the last analysis). They must be clear that it is not up to them simply to hand out judgments on the basis of a formal right as official teachers, but that they have also got to justify them as thoroughly as possible in terms of relevant argument, and that nowadays they have got to do this themselves and not merely leave it to other theologians. It is true that they are in a certain sense 'judges' with a formal authority (though of precisely what kind needs to be investigated and established in a way which is not being done from Rome), and thus not just theologians like any others, whose opinions depend on the worth of their arguments and hence can be disputed by other theologians with other arguments. The representatives of the teaching office do not only have the formal right to give decisions. There are situations in which it is their duty to do so, and not to keep on endlessly postponing the decision (sometimes for reasons of diplomacy and ecclesiastical politics which have nothing to do with the case), merely because unclarities remain and there is endless further scope for disputation. But the reasons given above do tell more today than ever before in favour of toleration on the part of the teaching office; a toleration called for by the nature of the case, by the human dignity of the theologian involved, and by the legitimate freedom of theology. I do not need to say more here than I sketched earlier on about the need and the means to give this kind of toleration on the part of the teaching office the guarantee and protection of institutional forms. Questions about how to practise and institutionalize toleration in the concrete lead naturally and inevitably to questions of practical judgment which can never be entirely settled by rational argument.

But the kind of case under discussion here also demands toleration on the part of the theologian concerned. That may sound odd. But it is so. In the first place, toleration requires a basic recognition of the authority of the teaching office, in its different degrees and its binding character, as taught in traditional fundamental theology and ecclesiology. Hence it also means that an individual theologian, however justified he may be in questioning the objective basis of a decision, past or present, given by an official teaching authority, should not behave as though he were dealing with someone on the same level as himself in a dispute between theologians. He has really got to respect the special character and authority of the teaching office, to 'tolerate' it. He has got to remain patiently and self-critically aware of his own fallibility. He has got to be honest in reckoning with the fact that his own opinion is that of one historically conditioned individual sinner; that limited vision, self-opiniatedness and egotism have contributed to it; that it is liable to be subtly infected by non-theological currents, limitations, fashions of his own time, so that while it is perhaps very modern, it may for that very reason be false to a truth preserved in the traditions of the past.

In my opinion, toleration of this sort on the part of a theologian involved in doctrinal conflict has another aspect as well, always supposing that one is willing to include what I mean under the heading of toleration. Modern theologians in danger of coming into conflict with the Church's teaching authority often lay stress on a legitimate pluralism in theology today. But the existence of this pluralism also implies that a theological opinion or dogma in the Church today can be approached and expressed in very different ways. But this again implies that a theologian cannot maintain that what he wants to say can only be accurately expressed in the form which is calling down on him the danger of being censored by authority for contradicting a dogma of the Church. A modern theologian must not only demand respect for theological pluralism from the teaching authority in the Church; he must practise it self-critically himself; that is, be self-critically flexible in respect of the formulations which he might otherwise prefer to use. This is not a matter of cowardly, conformist accomodation to official mentalities and formulas. It is rather a matter of legitimate sceptical relativism in respect of one's own opinions or their formulation, for the sake of peace in the Church and the preservation (so far as possible) of a common language in the Church as serving the unity of faith. A correct insight, perfectly compatible with dogma rightly understood, does not have to be formulated in such a way as to look like a blatant contradiction of a dogma, or even of the ecclesiastical rules of language unavoidably bound up with the expression of a dogma. If something true, though perhaps new, has been perceived, it surely can be said without giving bitter offence to the traditional expressions and forms of Church dogma. A modern theologian must be capable of more than one language-gaem, if he is convinced of the pluralism of theology today. If he wants, rightly, to introduce some new things to the common awareness of theology or even perhaps of faith, it is only a toleration of this sort which will enable him really to do so. Otherwise he remains an outsider, his opinions doomed to be rapidly overtaken by the next fashion in theology and forgotten. Toleration of this kind, meaning a relativizing of one's own opinions and a readiness to re-express them in a manner more readily intelligible to the Church's teaching authority, is a legitimate attitude in a self-critical theologian. It is an act of humility and peace-seeking towards the official authorities in the Church; an act which recognizes the historical character both of oneself and of the Church, neither of which is capable of achieving everything all at once; it expresses a right relationship towards the truth, which is ultimately something which can only be possessed in selfless, that is self-relativizing, love. Were more time available, all this could be illustrated and made clearer with examples from particular conflicts, but time is too short.

3. We come now to the cases where the theological opinion of an individual Christian theologian is not in direct and explicit conflict with any actual dogma, but with doctrines which the teaching office itself does not proclaim as dogma but nevertheless 'proposes' as binding: what are called 'authentic' statements of the magisterium. We cannot here go into details about the fact that there are such authentic doctrinal statements short of actual dogma; why they have been made, are made, and in principle may be made in the future; nor why, and in precisely what way, a theologian has got to approach these too with the requisite respect, and not simply down-grade them to theological opinions which his own opinion confronts on equal terms. These things will have to be taken for granted here. So will teaching on the fine gradations in the binding nature of such authentic doctrines, resulting from differences in the teaching authority concerned (pope, Roman congregations, bishop) and in the length of time and degree of emphasis with which such doctrinal statements have been made, and so on. Nor can we discuss, as is done as part of the traditional doctrine about the Church's teaching office, the different kinds of assent which Christians and theologians need to give to doctrinal statements of this sort. Just one point on this. In ordinary human life, not everything is an absolute conviction. There are also opinions, provisional judgments open to revision, judgments based on estimate and so on. There can be

similar degrees of assent to official, authentic teachings of the Church. It is not right to impose on the teaching office the alternatives of either making a binding definition or simply keeping quiet and leaving the question to discussion between theologians.

It is possible, according to the traditional teaching of the Church and its theologians, for the teaching office to err when making authentic declarations of this kind; according to the evidence of history, and also according, for instance, to a declaration of the German Bishops' Conference, such errors have frequently occurred, right down into our own century. We cannot give examples here because it would take too long. Here too toleration is called for from both parties to any possible conflict. First of all, the theologian and individual Christian must approach these statements, too, with tolerant good will and docility. He must think seriously and with an open mind about them and the reasons for them (which the teaching office, for its part, ought to give more clearly than it has in the past). After such a non-definitive but authentic official teaching has been given, he will not proceed with the dialogue exactly as though nothing had happened. He will seriously enquire into the motives, which may be of a much more binding character, at work behind the statement; he will take the full weight of these motives into account (they may be rooted in the very centre of the faith, even when the doctrinal statement itself remains questionable), and help those whom he teaches to understand them.

But nevertheless, in the cases in question the dialogue must go on; *silentium obsequiosum* is most emphatically not the one and only right attitude for a theologian faced with a doctrinal statement of this sort to which he cannot assent. A theologian's 'toleration' (if we may apply the word here) cannot go that far in all cases; especially if, as he carries on his critical dialogue with the teaching authority, he makes it clear that he does not regard his own teaching, either, as an infallible truth, but only as an opinion which needs further consideration and discussion. But this attitude needs to be more than a mere verbal acknowledgment at the beginning or end of the discussion. When an authentic official teaching is being subjected to further critical examination, this attitude must really inform the matter and manner of the discussion itself.

But in these cases, what is required above all is toleration on the part of the Church's teaching authority. It is capable of error; it may mingle truth with falsehood in its declarations; it may be shortsighted, over-anxious, narrow, and because of all this hamper the very thing it wishes to serve: the real truth and living power of the gospel. It seems to me that, speaking generally at any rate, it is no longer appropriate today for the teaching office to follow up a statement of this kind by forbidding further discussion, or demanding retractations from the representatives of contrary opinions, or trying to impose it by administrative measures like sacking people. Such measures seem to me inappropriate, at least nowadays and in general, because they do not achieve their object. The discussion goes on anyway, but it withdraws into places where the teaching authority cannot follow and observe it. Theologians become either anxious and timid or embittered and distrustful. They complain of unjustified restrictions on the freedom of their science; they feel that they are being treated like school-children by people whose competence they question; they feel that their intention is being impugned, though this remains the service of the gospel, the clarification of truth without which the life of the Church is impossible.

I cannot avoid the impression that section 25 of *Lumen Gentium*, when it demands 'religious submission of mind and will' to the Roman teaching office, even when the Pope is not exercising his supreme teaching authority, is not sufficiently nuanced (nor is what follows in the text) to do justice to this matter and to the toleration required of the teaching office today. To understand the demand for an increased practice of toleration on the part of Rome, in comparison with the past, there is also this to be considered: the intellectual situation is different today, it seems to me, from what it used to be. I think that in the past it was assumed (and normally more or less correctly) that when a theologian stated a particular position he was proposing it as 'certain', with a more or less absolute commitment to it; and that any of his readers who agreed with him would be adopting his position in a correspondingly definitive way. Today this has changed. In the relativist, sceptical, scientific mentality of our time there is the feeling that all opinions, including so-called scientific conclusions, are provisional, and that the real achievements of science have occurred through the falsification of hitherto established opinion. This mentality may have its limitations and dangers, but it is very widespread. Because of this, it seems to me that the teaching authority may, without anxiety, leave the opinions of theological science, even when it considers them false, to further theological discussion, and not jump to the conclusion that such positions are being put forward with all the seriousness of absolute decisions. Precisely because the modern scientific mentality is itself sceptical of science, and because science itself has to keep changing so fast, the teaching office should not be over-anxious about theological opinions, but have the courage to be tolerant and leave them to the free play of scientific forces. Moreover the history of Protestant theology shows how, in the absence of any precise teaching office, the power of the gospel itself continually works to restore orthodoxy.

In concrete individual cases it is not, of course, always easy to say whether something comes under this heading of conflict between a theologian and an authentic official teaching, or whether an actual dogma of the Church is involved, in which case fundamentally different principles apply, as already stated. When this is unclear, the teaching office would not be compromising itself or failing in its duty if it tolerantly waited for the theologians to argue the matter out; it might then become moderately clear whether there is really any conflict at the dogmatic level, whether objectively or in relation to the normal faith-consciousness of theologians and of the ordinary faithful (two things, not identical).

Again, in these conflicts over authentic but not definitive doctrines proposed by the official teaching authority, it is the task and duty of that authority, more the debate, arguing and campaigning in favour of the view it is convinced is correct, not being too quick with condemnations. The teaching office has ample resources for this, if only the Congregation for the Faith, rather than availing itself only of the services of a few Roman theologians, would call in other theologians from all over the world. In this connexion, no real co-operation between the Congregation for the Faith and the International Theological Commission at Rome has yet been worked out and institutionalized. The Congregation for the Faith still works too much in the manner of a secret tribunal; despite the data given in the *Annuario Pontificio*, its procedure, sources of information, responsible personnel and so forth are still far from being transparently open. Toleration, on the part of this body, would also include a greater measure of transparency. But officials have a tendency to become bureaucrats and protect themselves with secrecy. So toleration on the part of those below includes patience to endure the slow pace at which official bodies evolve. Being patient, of course, also means continually demanding, loud and clear, both the improvements in question and a faster rate of change.

III Practice and toleration

I come now to conflicts in the practical life of the Church, and the toleration they call for. I mean by these, all conflicts between Christians and ecclesiastical authority which are not directly concerned with the Church's doctrine. All sorts of such conflicts, over both issues and personalities, can and do occur in every area of the Church's life. Differences of opinion over the concrete structure of the liturgy, or Canon Law, or administration; personal clashes over appointments to ecclesiastical office, and so on. They can affect every level of the Church, right up to conflicts between the Pope and the synod of bishops, and they are probably more numerous than doctrinal conflicts, though in most cases they escape publicity.

I can say scarcely anything about all these cases here, since it is not possible to analyze the wide range of potential conflicts, very different in their nature and importance. Broadly speaking, I can only refer back to what was said in the first part about conflict and toleration in general, little and vague as it was. There is just one question on which to add something. Conflicts of this sort all have something to do with what is usually called ecclesiastical obedience; and obedience to his bishop is something to which a priest, at his ordination, makes an explicit commitment, specifically related to his office. There can be no doubt that, as something in the nature of obedience exists in every society, so it must, in a particular form, in the Church. This is so no matter what name we give to the readiness and determination to acknowledge and carry out legitimate decisions made by a higher authority; and no matter what greater precisions of theological interpretation we apply to the nature and dignity of the ecclesiastical organs of decision at the practical level.

There are without doubt numerous cases in which a subordinate, while doubting or disputing the correctness of a decision (and it is certainly the duty of authority to get its decisions right), cannot maintain that carrying out this decision would go against his moral conscience and thus oblige him to commit a sin. It may well be that even in Italy communion in the hand is today, objectively and in human terms, the better way to distribute communion. But no normal Italian parish priest could maintain that the rule of communion in the mouth compels him to commit a sin, so that he has to refuse. Normally, at least, a case like this calls for simple obedience. This still leaves one with the right, even perhaps the duty, to point out to those higher up, continually, boldly, and insistently, that their decisions are objectively at fault and that a change is called for. Normally, I said. For when dealing with the norms of practical living, which are for the most part based on discretionary judgments an individual, without seeking the prior approval of authority, can perfectly well have the right in an individual case to apply, freely and unihibitedly, the principle of *epikeia*[1] (including the teaching

[1] From the Greek *epieikeia*, equity; the name given in moral theology to a principle of interpretation of human laws. It means that such a law (even an ecclesiastical one) does not bind if right reason indicates that the legislator did not wish it to bind (in

111

about 'non-reception of a law by the people'). The principle of *epikeia*, as worked out by orthodox moralists and canonists, must not be allowed to remain a mere abstract theory.

But there are other cases as well. We must not pretend that it is not in practice possible in the Church for cases to arise in which authority, in all good faith, makes a decision which, in the judgment of a subordinate's conscience, can only be carried out with at least subjective guilt: either because what it obliges him to do seems to him to be sinful anyway, or because it would be in his particular case. Suppose that a subordinate in such a case does not see how he can avoid the application of such a decision by *epikeia*; or that he is convinced that he has got to reject this order outright, as conflicting with his own conscience. He has then the right and the duty not only to refrain, for his part, from carrying out the order, but also to make known his rejection of it, moderately but boldly and unambiguously. It is, generally speaking and in principle, the duty of the higher authority to respect this judgment of conscience: to practise toleration, if you like to use the word for this duty. It must not make any attempts of an illegitimate kind, injurious to the dignity of the conscience, to get the subordinate to reverse his judgment. It has a duty to shield him from consequent damage (as, for example, in case of unavoidable removal from office, transfer, alternative employment and so on. Toleration of this kind on the part of authority has got to emerge today as a real possibility.

these particular and quite concrete circumstances), for instance if the difficulty of obeying the law here and now were disproportionate to the end which the law has in view (thus St Thomas Aquinas, Suarez and others). (Quoted from *Concise Theological Dictionary*, by Karl Rahner and Herbert Vorgrimler, London, 1965).

The subordinate, for his part, has got to presume that authority has acted in good faith: that is, that it has taken its decision in accordance with its own well-instructed conscience. Hence he too has a duty to be tolerant; that is, to respect, as between human beings, the decision of conscience made by the higher authority. He has no right to be a wild revolutionary, not merely appealing to his own conscience against an individual decision of authority but speaking and acting in such a way as to dispute the very legitimacy of authority in principle or to endanger its capacity to function at all.

It is possible, of course, to conceive of a case in which authority, in all good faith, comes to the conclusion, which may be objectively or at least subjectively correct, that the subordinate's refusal to conform to a particular decision does imply a rejection of authority in principle and of the Church's necessary unity of practice. There is no need for this to be so in the majority of the cases envisaged here. But such a case is conceivable in principle, though to allow for it calls for the exercise of very great toleration and caution. Given that there really was such a case, we would have something analogous, at the level of practice, to the situation in which a Christian comes into conflict with the teaching authority of the Church over the dogmatic substance of the Christian faith. He could be regarded as a schismatic, and, in full respect for the decision of his conscience, he would have to be invited to leave the Church, even though in such a case there could be no dogmatic certainty that authority, in imposing this separation, was objectively right. Supposing that such an objectively incorrect expulsion were patiently accepted, we should then have, in the person thus separated *corpore* but not *corde* (to use Augustinian language) from the Church, about the most extreme possible case of toleration on the part of a Christian towards Church authority. Conflicts ought not to be hastily interpreted as of this kind, as, if I am not mistaken, did happen here and there a few years ago. But the case is not impossible. It too must be tolerated by those who hold office in the Church.

We seem to have talked of many things which have little or nothing to do with toleration in the Church. But if one is to talk about toleration without merely uttering vague, cheap exhortations, one has to talk about the different situations which, sometimes in quite different ways, call for something in the nature of toleration. It is only from such situations that it is possible to show what toleration in the Church at large could mean. So it is all to the good when it emerges that there is a wide range of people who have got to practise toleration and a variety of ways in which they have to do it; for example that toleration is not only something to be demanded of those who hold office.

However many different kinds of toleration have emerged in the course of this discussion, they all derive ultimately from one irremovable fact: within the ongoing course of human history, the different freedoms of human beings are ultimately irreconcilable with each other, and this fact has got to be accepted and endured with patience, that is, toleration. For even when the resolution of a conflict is in a way possible, and obviously must be striven for and attained to the limit of our powers, this still does not mean, taking a deeper and more radical view, that the ultimate and ultimately disparate freedoms involved have been reconciled. At best, a compromise has been reached, making the co-existence of these freedoms somewhat more 'tolerable'; but the Kingdom of reconciled freedoms in the full freedom of all freedoms is still an unfulfilled hope which belongs to eternity. Hence there are differences in the degree and the fashion in which this precarious and provisional co-existence of freedoms can be attained. And it is precisely this uneven co-existence of freedoms, achieving as much freedom and peace as possible, always provisional, always having to be patiently re-fashioned, which has to be accepted and endured in the hope of eternal reconciliation: which has, in a word, to be 'tolerated'.

Hence it is ultimately understandable that there can be cases (to be averted and kept within bounds by all possible means) when intolerance on both sides of a conflict cannot be avoided: the intolerance of a free conscience judging that it must not and cannot conform to a decision of authority in doctrine or practice; and the intolerance of the other side, unable to accommodate this decision within the Church. Such conflicts should be avoided to the utmost extent of our powers, but they are possible and may become actual in this ongoing history of humanity and the Church. When they happen, when they cannot be overcome, then they too must be accepted in patience. This is toleration, when human beings and the Church leave the final judgment to the eternal Lord of history, who does not delegate it to anybody: the Lord who alone will effect our final reconciliation at the end of history and give it to us; and then there will be no need of toleration any more.

Translated by Cecily Bennett